Praise for *24/6*

"*24/6* reminds us of what we get from taking a break rather than what we give up. Tiffany Shlain is a twenty-first-century Marshall McLuhan, reminding us that having the best of both worlds is not getting consumed by one."

—Jean Rogers, author of *Kids Under Fire*

"Shlain delivers a moving family story, documenting the connections that make the need for the Shabbat important in the first place."

—Sherry Turkle, author of *Reclaiming Conversation* and *Alone Together*

"She convinced me . . . that a day of disconnection is a path toward reconnection to the rest of our lives."

—Vint Cerf, vice president and chief Internet evangelist at Google and cofounder of the Internet Society

"Tiffany Shlain is a digital philosopher for our time. *24/6* proposes a simple but radical change in the power dynamic between humans and the Web. I, as a pediatrician, live it and recommend it as a best-parenting and best-living practice to the families I serve."

—Michael Rich, associate professor of pediatrics at Harvard Medical School and director and founder of the Center on Media and Child Health

"For decades the promise of automation—giving people more leisure time—has been a distant dream. The reality is quite the reverse. We may well need to relearn the art of leisure or how to fill more of our time with enriched personal and social relations. Tiffany Shlain's book is a much needed guide for how to start on this path."

—Marina Gorbis, author of *The Nature of the Future*

"I don't know how Tiffany Shlain does it. First the prize-winning movies, now an amazing book outlining a *human* way to manage our digital lifestyle. Like Tiffany, we all need to go 24/6. It's a great way to seize back control from our digital overlords."

—Andrew Keen, bestselling author of *How to Fix the Future*

"*24/6* is a joy to read, from its compelling argument for a day of rest to its bonus challah bread recipe. Like the braided challah, Tiffany Shlain weaves together her intriguing personal story, practical advice, and research wisdom to show why taking a weekly tech break is so rejuvenating—and can fuel a healthy, meaningful life."

—Rosabeth Moss Kanter, bestselling author of *Confidence*

"Tiffany Shlain provides much needed sanity in our data frenzied world. Do yourself a favor. Read this book and take back your life."

—Stephen Balkam, founder and CEO,
Family Online Safety Institute

24 / 6

THE POWER OF
UNPLUGGING
ONE DAY A WEEK

TIFFANY SHLAIN

GALLERY BOOKS
NEW YORK   LONDON   TORONTO   SYDNEY   NEW DELHI

G

Gallery Books
An Imprint of Simon & Schuster, Inc.
1230 Avenue of the Americas
New York, NY 10020

First Gallery Books hardcover edition September 2019

GALLERY BOOKS and colophon are registered
trademarks of Simon & Schuster, Inc.

For information about special discounts for bulk purchases,
please contact Simon & Schuster Special Sales at 1-866-506-1949
or business@simonandschuster.com.

The Simon & Schuster Speakers Bureau can bring authors
to your live event. For more information or to book an event,
contact the Simon & Schuster Speakers Bureau at 1-866-248-3049
or visit our website at www.simonspeakers.com.

Interior design by Michelle Marchese
Jacket design by John Vairo

Manufactured in the United States of America

10 9 8 7 6 5 4 3 2 1

Library of Congress Cataloging-in-Publication Data has been applied for.

ISBN 978-1-9821-1686-6
ISBN 978-1-9821-1688-0 (ebook)

To my parents, and Ken, Odessa, and Blooma,
my truest sources of connectivity

Contents

CONTENTS

CONTENTS

Introduction

Before living 24/6, I was on screens 24/7. While I loved the power of having the world at my fingertips, I felt powerless against the allure of the device in my hand. Screens both consumed most of my time and made me lose track of it. It was hard to focus while jacked into this primal-urge network that was constantly pulling me away from being present. Most important, I felt like I wasn't paying enough attention to the people I loved who were right in front of me.

Then, ten years ago, within days, my father left this world and my daughter entered it, and all I wanted to do was end the non-stop distractions and slow time down. I needed a revolution to transform the situation, and remarkably, I found it.

My husband, Ken, and I started a practice of turning off all screens and unplugging from digital life for a full day, every week, for what we call our "Technology Shabbat." Going offline one day a week for nearly a decade with our daughters has felt like an epiphany on how to fill the day with the best parts of life, and a radical act of protection against the always-on, always-available world.

Even though I'm Jewish and a mother, I'm not here to make you feel guilty (or become Jewish). I just want to share a practice that has improved my life in every way: a twenty-first-century interpretation of the ancient Jewish ritual of a weekly day of rest. It can work for anyone, from any background or belief, whether single, with a partner, or with kids. As concerns about the effects of excessive tech use on our individual well-being, our relationships, and our democracy come to a head, it's never felt more urgent to share this idea.

Living 24/6 feels like magic, and here's why: it seems to defy the laws of physics, as it both slows down time and gives us more of it. I laugh a lot more on that day without screens. I notice everything in greater detail. I sleep better. It strengthens my relationships and makes me feel healthier. It allows me to read, think, be more creative, and reflect in a deeper way. Each week I get a full reset. Afterward, I'm much more productive and efficient, with positive effects that radiate out to the other six days. It even helps renew my appreciation for all that I have access to online, giving me that *Wow, the Internet* realization fresh each week. Who would have thought technology could be more potent in its absence?

A weekly day without screens improves our family's lives, too. Our daughters, Odessa (sixteen) and Blooma (ten), have done this practice most of their lives, and it's shaped how they interact with technology in extremely beneficial ways. They enjoy their time off screens and look forward to it. It feels like a vacation every week. We look forward to it with the same anticipation, and it provides that same feeling of deep relaxation we get when we go away. And because it expands your sense of time, it makes your day off feel like two days in one. Going screen-free once a week is like having a metaphysical remote control, with a pause button for the 24/7 world, that turns your life back *on*.

The fact that my family has practiced Tech Shabbat so long surprises people. Ken is a UC Berkeley professor of robotics. I've spent my career exploring the online world, first by establishing the Webby Awards, then as a filmmaker examining how all this connectedness is changing our lives today and will continue to do so in the future. We're both deeply involved with technology and constantly pushing on its edge.

Yet what I'm exploring here is the power of a technology invented several millennia in the past. More than three thousand years ago, the concept of Shabbat (also known as the Sabbath) transformed the world. Before then, time had no pauses: it was day after day after day. Shabbat made it so each week ended with a day off, for everyone, of every social class. The run-on sentence of time got a period, and humankind got a chance to catch its breath and focus.

All these years later, practicing our version of Shabbat helps my family be more present with one another, appreciate the small things, daydream, and get a different viewpoint on living. It encourages resourcefulness and recalls a simpler time. Doing something the same day as others all over the world do also reminds us that we are connected to something larger than ourselves. Ultimately, turning off screens and disconnecting from the online network weekly helps us use tech in a way that prevents tech from using us.

If you're reading this book, you're probably looking for a change, too. How often have you looked up from your screen, eyes dazed, and realized you've just wasted thirty minutes or an hour or more? You look around and see everyone else with their heads down staring at their screens, too. You worry about how this is affecting you as an individual and society at large. You think you should do something about it, then your phone buzzes, you respond to the text, and you're pulled back to the screen again. We've become ostriches, burying our heads in silicon sand.

In 1876, when the inventor of the telephone, Alexander Graham Bell, made his first call, he said to his assistant on the other line: "Mr. Watson—come here—I want to see you." More than one hundred forty years later, with the proliferation of everyone staring at the screens of their smartphones 24/7, we might rephrase: "Humanity—come here—I want to see you." Having one day off each week shocks you anew into the realization of how bizarre it is that everyone is head-down, looking at screens all the time. That should never feel normal.

If you feel like screens rule too much of your life, living 24/6 offers a way to reclaim your attention, time, and perspective, and—if more and more people do it, I hope—will help our collective humanity.

I won't pretend there aren't costs in taking time off, or that it's easy for everyone. I know that having the space to think about time away from technology is a luxury that many don't have. It's true that in the past ten years, the digital divide has flipped, and now it's often a privilege to be able to be offline. You can't just unplug if you have to answer your boss's calls. And unlike the titans of Silicon Valley (many of whom created and deploy this addictive technology), who ban smartphones for both their children and the nannies who watch them, many of us rely on screens as child care when we absolutely need to get things done.

But there's still a cost to excessive screen use, and I want to share a practice that's free and simple and can make your life better. Yes, many people need to work seven days a week. But others have allowed themselves to be available seven days a week. Wherever you are, I urge you to try unplugging on the work-free days you do get, even if it's only doable every few weeks or every few months. If you are able, once a week is ideal. For me, it's restorative in a way that nothing else is.

Living 24/6 is a ticket to a richer life that coexists with technology in a more balanced way. The practices I suggest are for people of all backgrounds, and they don't follow the traditional rules of the Jewish Sabbath, like refraining from driving or using electricity. I should mention that I'm a cultural Jew, not a religious one (i.e., I love bagels, lox, cream cheese, and Gilda Radner, and I had a bat mitzvah). I value the traditions, the humor, the rituals, the food, the existential angst, and many key ideas, without necessarily believing in God. And while I have great appreciation for all the different ways my fellow Jews observe Shabbat, I don't view unplugging for a Technology Shabbat as just a Jewish practice. For me, Tech Shabbat is like yoga or meditation. I do both and respect the traditions they come from, but I don't think that doing them suggests I'm Hindu or Buddhist. These practices enhance your life whether you subscribe to that faith or not.

Because I am Jewish, I incorporate Jewish elements into my interpretation of Shabbat (like Friday-night dinner with challah and candles), and that's the tradition I'll be using to illustrate my practice throughout the book. But I appreciate the fact that people from different backgrounds honor their day of rest in other ways. So whatever your tradition, even if it's no tradition, take a day. Grab it and don't let it go. Your day away from screens and off the network will rejuvenate your mind, your body, and your relationships, whether you do it on Saturday, Sunday, or a weekday.

I see Tech Shabbat as part of a solution to a modern human problem. It breaks up the constant disruptions and rejects the status quo. Unplugging for a full day each week is a punk-rock reaction to our always-on, 24/7 world. It makes the world wait while we do what we want. It's totally freeing, and totally free.

While today unplugging means turning off screens, as technologies evolve and become more invisible—e.g., smart eyewear, microscopic earbuds embedded in home devices, and various forms of augmented reality—the core of what I'm talking about will remain the same: the need to turn off the online world for a full day each week and enter a different kind of space and time that allows for inner reflection, longer-term thinking, and more focused connection with your friends and family.

———————

To practice the same ritual almost every week for nearly ten years has changed me in ways both big and small. In this book, I will share my story and what I have learned from rethinking Shabbat for the twenty-first century.

The first sections offer context, looking at the history and philosophy that demonstrates why rest and unplugging are so important. After that, I'll show you what living 24/6 looks like, and how it can improve your life 24/7. Then I'll explore the shifting role of technology in our lives, looking at what it amplifies for us—and what it amputates. We'll look at the neuroscience behind productivity, practice, silence, sleep, empathy, and creativity, examining how they're enhanced by turning off screens. We'll consider what all this means for the bigger picture, and I'll propose some ideas for change for the tech industry and society.

The last section of the book, "It's Easier Than You Think: A Step-by-Step Guide," offers hands-on instructions for making these ideas work for your own circumstances. I have strategies to help convince the people you want to do this with you (a partner, kids, friends, or anyone), including thinking about what you all want more of in your life, so you can fill your screen-free day with those activities. There are lists of things to do, questions, prompts, and resources to help you tailor Tech Shabbat and living 24/6 to your own life, as well as strategies for more balance with tech the other six days of the week. You can also read firsthand accounts from people who have tried and adapted the practice themselves.

Ultimately, this book is a why-to and a how-to, not a have-to. (There are enough Commandments as it is.) 24/6 living is also a get-to: it's about what you get back, not what you give up. This is what's worked for us. You can customize to make it work for you.

I'm excited to share with you what I've learned so far.

To the power of unplugging and looking up,

Tiffany Shlain
2019

PART I:
A DAY DIFFERENT FROM
ALL OTHER DAYS

1

Why I Went 24/6

In 2008, Ken and I found out I was pregnant with our second child after multiple miscarriages. That same week, my father was diagnosed with stage-four brain cancer and given nine months to live. For the next nine months, all I thought about was life and death.

My father and I were incredibly close. We spoke every day, and although I saw him through more realistic eyes as I got older, most of my life I viewed him as a combination of Superman, Einstein, Willy Wonka, and Tevye from *Fiddler on the Roof*.

During the period when he was dying, there were times when he had only one lucid hour a day. When I went to visit him, I would turn my phone off completely. I needed to protect a space and time around us to focus on him and the moments we had left.

This made me think a lot about how little time we actually have. One of my favorite quotes by author Annie Dillard is: "How we spend our days is, of course, how we spend our lives." I was spending too much of my days looking at screens. I no longer wanted to spend every waking moment being sucked into the digital vortex.

It's stunning how sickness and death can jolt priorities into alignment. Those nine months were painful yet illuminating. I was fully awake and present—both to my father's dying and this new life growing inside of me.

In May 2009, my father died, and Ken's and my second daughter was born. These events seemed to unfold in slow motion and in deeply saturated colors and emotions. I described the colliding of these two profound moments as a six-word memoir:

Father's funeral. Daughter's birth. Flowers everywhere.

At my father's funeral, over and over people told me: "Your father made me feel like the most important person in the room." "He was so present." "He always looked in my eyes when we spoke."

I remember growing up, how he never answered the landline when it rang at dinnertime. "Who has the nerve to call during dinnertime?" he would say. "Family time is sacred." To him, interrupting the family meal was an assault on the most important event of the day. The fact that his death occurred just as our smartphones began to take over all our waking hours is more than just significant; to me, it felt like that's when "being present" died—for all of us.

———

My father was the reason I met Ken. On a rainy night in 1997, my father was giving a reading of his book *Art & Physics* at an art gallery in San Francisco. A dashing man walked through the door of the gallery with a dog-eared copy and said to my father,

2 4 / 6

"Hello, Dr. Shlain, my name is Ken Goldberg. I'm a professor at UC Berkeley, and I loved your book."

I can imagine the mental checklist going through my father's head:

1) Goldberg, Jewish: Check.
2) Professor, smart: Check.
3) Loves my book: Check!

Without missing a beat, my father walked Ken over to me, asking, "Have you met my daughter Tiffany?" We fell in love instantly.

Ken introduced me to the idea of Shabbat as a weekly break from work. Most Jews I knew did not observe Shabbat, or if they did, it was just candles, blessings, and a nice meal on Friday night. I remember so clearly being shocked when he said, "I don't work on Saturdays; it's Shabbat. I need a day off." I was impressed. It struck me as profound and sexy. I was drawn to how much this ancient Jewish wisdom guided him.

During our first ten years together, Ken and I were focused on creating a life and a family, and also on our careers. This meant we were really busy—and on our screens a *lot*. But that was a time when screens were mostly stationary. Until smartphones were released around 2007, we couldn't plug in anywhere, anytime. (It's hard to remember how different things were.) Back then, it was pretty much just flip phones and the Palm Pilot. Remember those original models with a screen and cool little pull-out stylus that let you both make a call *and* keep a calendar? The Palm Pilot was a huge leap from the oversize bricks that came before.

And that was nothing compared to the moment when that device turned into a computer + a mobile phone + access to the Web. Now, everyone was online all the time.

I clearly remember the night we took the iPhone plunge in 2007. I tried to convey to Ken why I worried that smartphones might be a detriment to our relationship. But, of course, we opened our white Pandora's boxes from Apple and started mainlining data, texts, emails, and calls like everyone else. We could bring our screens with us everywhere, and we did. We now had these intoxicating, compelling devices in our pockets, ready for a hit of distraction, entertainment, or escape at any moment.

And like everyone else, we got addicted. Researchers have compared the sense of technological dependency—the feeling that we must be accessible and responsive at any time—to that of drugs and alcohol. It's all because of the hormone dopamine, which is related to mood, attention, and desire. When you find something that feels good, dopamine makes you want more of it. I recently heard the term "digital obesity." Yes, I get it. Too much of anything can be detrimental to your health and well-being.

When you're up late, clicking from website to website, or compulsively texting or emailing, it's reinforcing dopamine-induced loops. And just as we've discovered the hard way when we have too much sugar or too much alcohol, we can also have too much information: literally TMI. But back when the iPhone first came out, we couldn't imagine how much it would encroach on our lives. We thought we could stop scrolling and clicking whenever we wanted to.

Unfortunately, that's not how human brains work. Within a year of its release, everyone around me seemed addicted to their smartphones. My attention span got shorter. I felt distracted all the time. I was more available to everyone and connected to everything, but not in a meaningful way. This was at the time of my father's health crisis, and I was doing a lot of thinking about thinking. Specifically, I was thinking about the brain, and how it responds when it's attacked or in an unhealthy situation.

My father, Leonard Shlain, was a surgeon and writer whose work focused on the brain. At the time of his illness—which, in a painful irony, was brain cancer—he was working on his last book, *Leonardo's Brain: Understanding da Vinci's Creative Genius*. He finished the book days before he died. Attention and mindfulness would be important to anyone in that situation, but to him—an author who had spent a lot of time considering the evolution of the brain and communication—they were especially so.

A short time after my father's death in 2009, an organization that Ken and I belong to called Reboot asked us to participate in a collective day to rethink the Sabbath for our modern age called the National Day of Unplugging. For the occasion, the two of us rewrote Allen Ginsberg's "Howl" as a modern takedown of our tech-addicted society ("I saw the best minds of our generation distracted by texting, tweeting, emailing!"). At that point, Ken and I had been doing partial versions of Shabbat, but those screens always pulled us in and out of being together. The abridged form just wasn't enough.

We were ready for something bigger. While Reboot's plan was for one full day offline annually, the experience made us feel so good and present that we decided to continue the practice weekly. We called it our "Technology Shabbat" because we combined a screen-free twenty-four hours with some Shabbat rituals, like a special Friday-night meal with family and friends. We had no idea how many years we would continue this weekly Tech Shabbat ritual or how much it would change our lives.

We also had no idea ten years ago how crazy everyone would become with their screen obsessions. Our 24/7 society is a fire hose of media, news, emails, tweets, posts, likes, texts, pings, notifications, and buzzes. We all need a break. This weekly boundary we created around our life not only reconnected us but also enriched our time and space.

I mean this literally. For many, and definitely our family, the day means treating the house and nature like a sacred space. In his seminal book, *The Sabbath*, the twentieth-century Jewish philosopher Abraham Joshua Heschel writes, "The seventh day is a palace in time *that we build*" (italics mine). *We* have to create it, brick by brick, detail by detail. There is the specialness of how we set the table. We invite over friends, family, or new people we want to know better. We perform our own version of the Shabbat rituals. I have always loved the line from author Stephen R. Covey, "I think the most significant work we'll do in our whole life, in our whole world is done within the four walls of our home."

———————

Here's what our house is like Friday evenings as we prepare to close the door on the network and the nonstop world. The smells of rosemary, garlic, onions, chicken, and baking challah fill the house. All the piles of papers and books and laptops that normally lay claim to the kitchen table are put away, and the table is set with a tablecloth, candles, and freshly cut flowers. Before the guests arrive, everything gets powered down. The whole night is like a slow exhalation to end the week.

If you're imagining one of those perfect families that eats dinner together every night, that's not us. Ken and I both need to travel for work, and we tag-team when he's teaching late or I am working long hours on a film. In reality, we all eat together as a family two to three nights during the week. After all the weekday craziness, this grounding Friday-night dinner resets and frames our week for our family.

It takes a little bit to adjust. Sometimes on Friday night, I have the phantom-limb sensation of reaching for a smartphone that isn't there, to look something up or check email. So I keep paper and a black Sharpie out on the kitchen counter and jot down whatever combination of to-dos, reminders, questions, or ideas that tumble from my head. Then I feel set free, with a full twenty-four hours of time and space to think and be. In this palace, we're walled off from distractions, temptations, pings, and obligations. We laugh more. We're looser. More engaged.

The sleep of Friday night is the most delicious deep sleep of the week. We usually go to bed shortly after our friends and family leave. There are no Siren screens to seduce us.

Because we have gone to bed early and slept well, Ken and I wake up early, before the kids. We enjoy a leisurely morning over coffee, reading, and writing in journals.

Saturday morning, I'm prepared. I've already printed out the schedule the day before and placed it next to a coffee-stained sheet of phone numbers on the counter that used to just live on my cell phone. Friends and family know they will not be able to text, email, Facebook, or FaceTime with us for twenty-four hours; if they need to get in touch, they'll have to call the landline or come by the house.

Your schedule may be more structured, and that can work, too. Some people say, "We have so many events on Saturday, how would I coordinate with people?" My answer is to print out a schedule and make a plan on Friday afternoon. It's amazing how we were all able to survive prior to smartphones. When we do have a plan with others, we just pick a time and place to meet, and then we meet them, without all the text exchanges: *I'm running late. I'm parking. 2 mins away.* Do we really need that blow-by-blow account of everyone's journey? We usually say "We'll be there" or "We'll be a little late."

With some advance planning it's easy to go phone-free, even if your Saturdays are busy, as ours sometimes are when the girls both have soccer games. Not taking our phones actually makes these days feel less hectic, too, because we stick to set plans, we're not being interrupted, and we can focus on what we're doing in the moment.

What if people need to get in touch with us in case of an emergency? We have a landline for just that purpose. (And in all the years we have been practicing this ritual, really only our family members call on that line, and mostly, it doesn't ring at all.)

What about the emails, the voice mails, the texts that pile up? They'll still be there the next day, and in ten years, I've hardly ever missed something important because I took twenty-four hours to recharge and respond. Alerting people in your life and at work that you're taking a day off to rest and recover is a positive example to set.

What if your work is too important to take a day off? Remember that well-being is important, too, and that you can't do your best work if you don't take care of yourself.

What if you can't afford to take the day off? A weekly day off may not be possible right now. When you do get time away from work, even if it's every few weeks or less often, give yourself a true rest by not spending it on screens.

When people first learn about our Tech Shabbat, their reaction is usually one of disbelief—*You can do that?*—as if we need permission. It's incredibly freeing to realize you have the power to turn it all off.

Some people say to me, "My teenage kids would never do it." But you are the parent. You can make anything happen. Parenting is about modeling behavior. Insisting that there will be one day a week without devices and knowing that we will have more authentic connection with one another without screens, more time to just be and think in a different way, delivers a powerful message. And whether our kids realize it or not, they need that time offline, too.

If you are single or child-free, just think how much you'd prefer your Saturday as a day focused on friends, relationships, health, and hobbies rather than wondering what you might have missed or stressing about work. I recall how meaningful it was to Ken as a single young adult.

If you don't think you can get your partner to agree because they're glued to their phone, this is pretty hard evidence that they need to unplug more than anyone. I will share strategies to get them on board. Once they are, I doubt they'll want to go back.

The point is, you can come up with a lot of reasons not to try it. But I've found that there are many more compelling reasons why you should. Things will come up, and you'll need to make adjustments; life can be messy and we are all only human. However, what you gain by having this practice in your life is transformative. Our Tech Shabbat is a force field of protection that gives us the strength, resilience, perspective, and energy for the other six days. It lets us achieve the balance we need to live in both the online world and real life. It is our favorite day, and we look forward to it all week.

That's how it goes every week. Of course, there are times each year when we can't pull it off (work or family travel, a big deadline), but that rarely happens. When it does, it makes me feel unmoored. I'm more "orthodox" and almost never break the tradition; Ken, who hates strict rules, will bend it more, because that's what works best for him. You'll find your own balance.

A person has an average of thirty thousand days on this earth. I discovered the power of practicing Tech Shabbat around fifteen thousand days into my journey. I'm so glad I did. Wherever you are on your path, it's never too late. Living 24/6 brings back balance, resets your focus, and gives you the space to think about how you want to live your life.

So even though it may never feel like a good time to start unplugging, now is the best time. Let's get started by considering the origins of a day of rest.

2

A Brief History of a Day of Rest

The arrival of digital technology has completely changed how we view time, how we structure it, and, often, how we have lost control of it. In the process we've created a culture where we're almost never fully off duty, and even leisure time, when it must be carefully staged for Instagram, can be exhausting. We need to reclaim our time off. As history shows, few things are more important.

When the day of rest originated, it changed the world. It began several thousand years ago when an ancient desert tribe, the Hebrews, started observing a weekly day of rest they called Shabbat, or Sabbath, which was enshrined as the Fourth Commandment. The fact that a few people just put down their plows and took a day off might not sound like much, but it was huge.

First of all, it's what actually gave us the week. Without a day off, how did anyone know when one set of days ended and another began? It was endless day after day after day. Shabbat gave us defined times. There was sacred time, and there was regular time. There was time to work, and there was time to rest and recover, to connect and do the big-picture thinking that drives culture forward.

Shabbat redefined time and how we spend it. Over the coming millennia, other cultures as well as civil groups would develop similar observances. The need to pause and recharge is universal; most religions have some form of rest day. For Christians, it's Sunday. For Muslims, Friday became a day for communal worship and family time, and Buddhists observe periods of rest and communal worship called Uposatha. During the new moon, the Cherokee traditionally abstained from work for a period known as "non-days" or "un-time." In the nineteenth and twentieth centuries, secular movements, like labor unions, would call for much-needed days off as well.

So how exactly did this concept come about? Some scholars believe the Sabbath was originally observed monthly, on the full moon, rather than weekly, and was a day of worship, rather than rest. The name may come from *sa-bat*, full moon or "midrest" in Sumerian, or *shap battu*, "fifteenth day" in the Semitic Akkadian language.

At some point, however, Shabbat became a joyous, communal event that took place every seventh day, and the seven-day week was born. Why seven days? That's not entirely clear, either, but seven was a meaningful number in the ancient world, often signifying fullness and completion, as suggested by the Old Testament creation story. It would catch on in a way that longer and shorter weeks never would. No one remembers, for instance, that the ancient Egyptians had a ten-day week. As for ancient Romans, their week was eight days long, with one day designated as a market day. Instead of keeping a Sabbath, they kept a *Shoppath*.

The Sabbath changed again when the Jews went into exile. What had been a practice centered around a place—the Temple—now became a practice centered around a time. If they couldn't gather at a specific place, they would now gather at a specific time to observe specific rituals.

Once Shabbat came to mean a communal, recurring seventh day of rest and worship, it started producing big cultural changes. In ancient times, it would highlight the importance of astronomy: if a given day was sacred, you needed to know when that day began and ended (defined by the position of the stars; even today, the traditional Jewish Shabbat ends when three stars are visible in the sky) and when that day occurred (defined by the phase of the moon).

In a time of widespread servitude, the Sabbath was an early call for labor rights as well as class equality, as the Fourth Commandment made clear it was a day off for everyone. It created time for education, for worship and reflection, and for the thoughtful contemplation that leads to creativity. It allowed time to build family bonds, both metaphorically and very literally: it was a double mitzvah (Hebrew for "a good deed"), the rabbis said, for married couples to have sex on Shabbat. Which brings us to the next quality Shabbat must include: joy. The Sabbath was, by biblical decree, to be a "delight."

Later, Christian sects like the Puritans would embrace the Sabbath too. The Sabbath fit well with their overall work ethic (since the command to rest one day was complemented by the need to work the other six). In her book *The Sabbath World*, culture critic Judith Shulevitz posits that the Sabbath would lead, in part, to the founding of the United States, pointing out that one of the reasons Puritans left Europe and settled in America was because Europeans didn't observe the Sabbath strictly enough.

The Puritan Sabbath was definitely strict. According to legend, in 1789, President George Washington himself was stopped by an official for riding his horse on the Sabbath, a violation of New York state laws. Washington got off with a warning when he explained that he was riding to church.

When the Industrial Revolution came along (1760 to 1840), catapulting the West into an age of mass production and efficiency, ideas about work and time changed again. Modernization was gathering steam—literally, as steam engines connected points across the continents. This brought big changes to the concept of "time." Americans and Europeans had been telling time by clocks, rather than the sun, but the clocks weren't synced. For the trains to run on time and not run into each other, everyone had to agree what time it was. Local, unregulated time zones needed to be made uniform. For the first time in history, time became standardized. Greenwich Mean Time was adopted across the United Kingdom in 1847; and in North America, American and Canadian railways would establish time zones in 1883.

It's hard enough making plans now; imagine what it was like a couple hundred years ago. It must have made for some awkward love notes: "Dearest Hortense, let us meet at the bell tower the moment the spire's shadow hits the fourth spittoon from the left. If the day be cloudy and without shadow, we'll rendezvous at the apothecary when the town crier makes his rounds, lest drunkenness makes him tardy, in which case, we meet another day."

During that same period, there was a popular campaign to use the Christian Sabbath, Sunday, to learn and explore, a controversial concept for those who believed it should be devoted to worship. But the practice caught on and spread, and is the reason that museums and libraries eventually started opening on Sundays in the late 1800s.

The Industrial Revolution also precipitated the arrival of some hugely important labor practices that remain in place today. The biggest change was the full weekend: around the turn of the twentieth century, there was a proposal to give workers not just one day of rest but two (which they needed, to recover after five consecutive fifteen-hour days toiling in poorly ventilated factories). Labor unions began demanding eight-hour workdays and forty-hour workweeks, a fight that resulted in bloody battles on the streets of Chicago. The forty-hour workweek became more and more common after Henry Ford instituted this schedule in 1914. His motives weren't entirely pure—he hoped his employees would use their time off buying and driving Ford automobiles— but the upshot was good for everyone. (Though it's certainly ironic that the anti-Semitic Ford's big innovation of rest days was actually invented by the Jews.)

As mentioned earlier, one of the most interesting things about the Fourth Commandment is that you're not just told to *take* Shabbat off; you're told to *give* Shabbat off. It's a day of rest not just for the head of the household but for every member of it, including all the workers. Even the livestock get a break. Thousands of years before our current concerns about animal rights and growing economic disparities, the ancient Hebrews established a way to make everyone equal, every week. As the Unitarian minister Ana Levy-Lyons writes, this is where Heschel and Karl Marx overlap: "time is the ultimate form of human wealth on this earth. Without time, all other forms of wealth are meaningless. It is this insight about time—patently obvious but frequently forgotten— that makes keeping a Sabbath day both spiritually profound and politically radical. To reclaim time is to be rich."[1]

Importantly, everyone got the *same* day off. The value of this became apparent in the early Soviet Union, when Stalin got rid of weekends altogether in 1929. Under the program of *nepreryvka* ("continuous workweek"), weeks would now be five days long, and days off would be staggered. You might rest on day one, while your spouse rested on day three and your parents on day four. The idea was that this would let factories run continuously, with the side benefit of preventing church attendance or family gatherings. Even though the new schedule meant workers actually got more days off—seventy instead of fifty-two each year—people *hated* it. Because . . . everyone was out of sync.

Another thing happens when people come together: they get ideas. This was a big part of the reason Stalin instituted *nepreryvka*. When people didn't have time off together to reflect and brainstorm, they couldn't come up with notions that would challenge the state; they couldn't organize any kind of cohesive rebellion. It was hard just to organize relationships. But a culture needs those common days of work-free reflection, to undertake activities both idle and vital. We languish without it.

Revolutions bring upheaval. Though we may not realize it, we're currently in the middle of our own, and we're only beginning to understand its impact on our conception of time. Unfortunately, in some ways, this revolution is turning the clock back to an earlier time. Many of us don't get weekends off anymore: a recent study found that 63 percent of people say their employers expect them to do some work on most weekends.[2] People have always been busy, but there used to be more downtime. There used to be more structured beginnings and endings to days. You would only read news once or twice a day—a morning or evening newspaper. You could go to bed with a book instead of work emails. You would really go on vacation (without a laptop and cell phone so everyone couldn't get to you). You would take a walk in the woods without your phone. Now we get input from everywhere, every waking moment.

Meanwhile, research is making it clear that working extra days isn't just bad for employees, it's bad for companies. Over time, an employee working sixty hours a week will actually produce *less* than an employee working just forty hours. An overworked employee is also upping their risk of heart disease and early death. We've retained the Puritans' Protestant work ethic, but not their commitment to an ironclad day off.

The right to two days off each week has been around for only a hundred years or so, and a lot of people campaigned tirelessly to establish it. We need it. We earned it. So why are we giving it up so easily?

24/7 technology is bad for us and bad for the culture. We rush to fill any unstructured moment we have with work and entertainment, feeds and updates, pulling out devices that distract us from bigger-picture thinking. We're constantly reacting and responding without reflection. We've created a culture where we've all but relinquished our free time. We need to reclaim it.

While two days off every weekend is great, even one screen-free day a week can restore our palace in time—the special, designated hours that used to simply be the norm. Only thirty years ago, you couldn't do your banking after five. You could watch cartoons only on Saturday morning. You couldn't order a giant inflatable unicorn at three in the morning and probably didn't realize how much you needed to do that. But now you can watch *anything* twenty-four hours a day. You can buy anything, make anything, do almost anything anytime. And because we can do anything anytime, we feel we need to do everything all the time. With so much constantly available and streaming, we're constantly being sucked in.

During the Industrial Revolution, experts predicted that all the technological advances would make work so efficient that workers would need to work only four hours a day. What happened? Today we have less free time, lower levels of happiness, and more stress. And we're too busy and distracted to change. We need something different.

That's exactly what a day of rest, unplugged from the network, offers. Because that's another part of Shabbat: it evolves. For most of my life I thought a full day off for Shabbat was only for religious Jews, and it had to be done in a very specific way. It didn't feel accessible to me. But eventually, I realized I could engage with it and make it work for me. And I'm not the first to do this.

The Commandment to keep Shabbat may be carved in stone, but the way people have observed it isn't. From biblical times to now, every generation has adapted it to suit the age, and even the most traditional observation of the Sabbath is very different than it was three thousand years ago. Every tradition was once an innovation. Let's use this modern twist on an ancient idea to make a new one.

3

The Technology of Rest

"Labor is a craft, but perfect rest is an art."

—ABRAHAM JOSHUA HESCHEL

The promise of technology is that it makes things efficient. It saves time, and it allows us to get things done. Rest does, too. So what if we started thinking of *rest* as a technology? Though it's incredibly simple—it literally requires you to do nothing—rest is actually one of the most effective technologies there is. Sleeping eight hours a night, for instance, can dramatically increase your efficiency. Taking a full *day* of rest every week increases it even more.

By giving you a complete day off each week from screens, from obligations, from being available, letting you reflect and connect, Tech Shabbat becomes the ultimate technology to make you the most creative, present, and productive version of yourself. It's like a system update to keep you running in our always-on world.

It's sort of ironic: by doing nothing, you accomplish more. Ken discovered this when he was in his early twenties. In his words: "I started using Shabbat as a form of self-defense during graduate school. I spent six months in Israel, where Shabbat is the law. No buses, no movies, no shops, nothing to do. So I made the best of it. I read poetry and philosophy, I painted, I listened to my cassette player, I wrote in my journal, I walked, and I stared at the sky and daydreamed. I loved it. After a few weeks I started to look forward to these Saturdays. Sunday is a workday in Israel, and when I was on the bus heading back to the university, I felt very refreshed and excited to get back to work. I discovered that in most cases I was so productive on Sunday that it was as if I'd worked all weekend. Shabbat became my shield from the relentless pressures of studying and doing research. When I returned to Pittsburgh that fall, I continued the tradition. In my version of Shabbat, it was okay to talk on the phone, turn on lights, drive, or see a show, as long as it was for fun and not for work."

That resonated with me. I loved learning how Shabbat both gave him a day to hang out and increased his productivity. And it made me nostalgic for the Sundays of my childhood, when all stores would be closed, making the day feel special and distinct.

So many people tell me they don't have time to take a full day off every week from screens. I felt that way, too. So I was shocked to find that taking that one day off actually let me get *more* done by making me more focused and productive the other six. I didn't start unplugging for productivity but rather to be more present, but this added benefit is real.

Going 24/6 is also one of the best things I've ever done for running a company. When I was building the Webbys or starting my film studio, I spent years working what felt like 24/7. And so did my team. It's a reality for a lot of people and industries, and my team and I were no different. But since I've been doing Tech Shabbat for nearly a decade, things have changed.

It didn't happen overnight. But looking back over the years, I see a profound difference. Once I started turning off screens and not checking email from Friday to Saturday night, my team knew I was signing off, and they began to do the same. After a while, the culture at our studio changed. We, as an organization, are not expected to work on weekends. There are maybe one or two weekends a year when that's not the case—with enough warning and other time or benefit compensation—but as long as I'm off work on the weekend, my team is, too, with no expectation of correspondence. And just as my own productivity increased, so did my whole organization's.

Now we also limit our smartphone use during the workday. (Most of my team works remotely much of the time so when we are at our film studio all together, I am getting more serious about the time together being focused, with phones away, except for breaks. If we need to make a call or check something on the phone, we leave the room.) It's baffling how much personal distraction is interwoven into the modern workday. No wonder you're working ten hours a day; you can't get anything done when everyone is texting, tweeting, notifying you all day long. One study showed that it takes twenty-three minutes to recover from disruptions like your phone at work.[3] (Knowing this has definitely cut down on the number of texts I send out during the workday.) We are losing a *lot* of time.

Living 24/6 has given me a new perspective. I was too lost

in the go-go-go, do more-more-more. And now I am seeing that slowing down, being smarter with my and my team's time, and making every hour count is far more productive. And it's more meaningful. So yes, there has been greater output, but much more significant to me is that the output is more substantive.

For so long, tech and start-up "campuses" offered so many amenities that employees would never want to leave. Perhaps now we need to institute more time-balance principles. Some companies are already starting to. Time away from work is protected and understood as a way of increasing productivity, reducing burnout, and raising the quality of life of employees *and* employers. That means not sending stressful emails or planning high-stakes meetings on Friday afternoons that could ruin the weekend. Let's not text or call on the weekend unless it's really urgent information. Let's urge management to honor weekend time, knowing that time off will return value with dividends.

A 2014 study from Stanford on "The Productivity of Working Hours" showed that the relationship between productivity and hours worked is nonlinear, with productivity actually decreasing over fifty work hours per week. Companies that have offered employees thirty-two-hour workweeks, or six-hour workdays, report that their workforce gets more done while remaining happier in their jobs. Switching the perpetual motion machine to a lower gear means it breaks down less often.

Do you ever feel similar to the spinning wheel of doom that appears on your computer to tell you that you have too many programs active and the CPU is running hot? I sometimes feel like that computer: I have too many things going on at once, too many tabs opened, and my soul is overheating. (When I am talking to a good friend and we have so many things to talk about,

I say, "We have too many tabs open!") Like my laptop, my brain needs the occasional rest and reboot. Nothing is better for your computer or your body than a complete shutdown and restart. Each. Week.

Taking time off also means you have more time not just to rest but to *sleep*, which is essential to productivity, too. I know part of the reason I'm so productive after I plug back in is because I've slept so well on Shabbat. I often manage an afternoon nap as well, something I could never do during the week.

The restorative effects of rest are especially important for adolescents, who tend to stay up later, due to the delayed melatonin release of the teenage brain, and get up earlier, due to early high school start times. When a Seattle high school pushed back its start time, letting students get an average of thirty-four more minutes of sleep a night, their final grades in biology increased by 4.5 percent.[4]

Though researchers don't always agree on *why* sleep is so important, everyone concurs that it is. Sleep does so much for our bodies and our brains. It's when the pit crew comes in and gets everything ready for the next day.

One of the things that happens is a literal brainwash. While we're asleep, our brains actually shrink in a process called "synaptic homeostasis." This process makes room for the brain's level of cerebrospinal fluid to rise dramatically, washing out the damaging proteins that have built up over a day of thinking. It also allows synapses, which grow and widen while the brain is awake and busy but cannot grow indefinitely, to return to their normal size.[5]

While we're asleep our brains are also organizing information in ways that help us solve problems. During REM sleep all the information the brain took in during the day gets moved to the brain's memory center. There it gets filed next to existing memories . . . and sometimes forms connections that hadn't existed before. Which is why you're more likely to solve a problem after you've gone to sleep. As Thomas Edison said: "Never go to sleep without a request to your subconscious."

Edison, Albert Einstein, and Salvador Dalí all recognized that sleep spurred their creativity, and developed a similar practice to harness it. They would put something heavy in their hand (Edison used steel balls, Dalí and Einstein, a key) and sit in a chair. When they grew drowsy and relaxed, they would drop the object and wake up. That's when they felt like they came up with their biggest creative ideas (and perhaps broken toes).

It would be several decades later before researchers understood why this works. While we're awake, lots of information and ideas are flowing through our subconscious. We're not even aware of a lot of it. And sometimes, as we're drifting off, one of these thoughts will pop through. If we're lucky, it's a good one.

Dreaming can do something similar. We're still not sure exactly why we dream, but Harvard psychologist Deirdre Barrett theorizes that dreams are like a dress rehearsal that let us run scenarios from life, trying out different solutions.[6] Because the dreaming brain makes connections more quickly, we're apt to find solutions that elude us when we're awake. This definitely happens for me. When I'm stuck on something, sleeping on it often resolves the problem. Sometimes the answer comes in the middle of the night, so I keep a pen and paper by my bed to jot down ideas.

When we're young, we sometimes skip sleep, pulling all-nighters, without too many consequences, or so we think. Now I know this isn't very productive, and that my best work comes not from sleep deprivation but from a good eight hours of sleep, and not from being constantly on the go but from taking a day off of screens every week. After I've had a full day of rest, it's like a dam breaks; recharged and reinvigorated, I'm at my most productive and creative. The one day off to rest and think makes me reinvigorated to engage the world with a new perspective.

Recently, Netflix CEO Reed Hastings was asked who the company's biggest competition is. The answer? Not Amazon or HBO. He said, "We're competing with sleep." There was no great temptation to stay up until one in the morning when the only thing on was infomercials. But now we can bring screens right into our beds and binge-watch full seasons of shows. No wonder we're exhausted.

Work done by Dr. Larry Rosen suggests that having screens in the bedroom has results more dangerous than just fatigue—it also affects brain function. Lack of sleep, which can be caused by blue light from screens, creates higher buildup of beta amyloid plaque in the brain—something also seen with Alzheimer's.[7] We may be losing a lot more than sleep.

Living 24/6 actually makes *rest* the technology—the tool—that balances the encroachment of other technologies. By setting off a day of rest and reflection without screens, we can understand ourselves without the distractions of . . . everything. If we are online all the time and available to everyone with no time for quality rest, deep thinking, or real-world connecting, we aren't operating at our most efficient level. Unplugging becomes a tool that returns the power to you. It's good for your health, for your thoughts, for far-reaching ideas.

These are the things that 24/6 allows space and time for. While we rest, our bodies and minds are accomplishing much more than we realize. If we don't wind down, we'll never truly wake up.

PART II:
BEING ON 24/7

4

The Joys of Tech

It's no mystery why we're on our smartphones too much: they are *amazing*. Everywhere we go, we have this little device in our pocket that can answer any question, connect us to anyone or anything on the planet, order us lunch, count our steps, and bring a car right to the door. The future is truly here, and it's in a rose-gold shatterproof case.

There are countless examples of how technology can make life better, from collaborating with someone across the globe to microfinancing a life-changing venture we first saw online. We have access to all the world's information and can add to it, dispute it, and evolve it in real time. We can share information that actually saves lives: crowdsourcing medical solutions and connecting people with help after disasters. Socially isolated people can find community.

Technology has led to huge real-world advances. People are better educated and healthier than ever before. There are one billion people in the world who are disabled, and technology offers many of them the access and tools to participate in areas that were closed off before. As economists such as Martin Ravallion have shown, extreme poverty worldwide has declined sharply in the last twenty years. Americans' standard of living is the highest it's ever been.

Of course, all that growth has come with a downside. Sharply rising financial inequality since the 1970s has corroded democracy and economic growth by transferring wealth and power to a very small section of the population. And while technology may eventually help reverse it, as things now stand, climate change is a real and terrifying problem we haven't come close to facing, much less solving. The wrong people can get access to all the information we have given away freely and use it in nefarious ways. Getting our minds around the extent to which our data is manipulating us should give us deep, profound pause. There are many other technologies whose consequences we don't yet fully grasp. On a personal level, I worry about how it's affecting our mental health and relationships, as the growing backlash against technology (techlash) suggests.

The irony, of course, is that technology is what makes this backlash possible. We worry about Facebook . . . on Facebook. We read articles about spending too much time online . . . while we're online. We can't seem to get away from it. We're always being distracted or texted or tweeted *at*, and every notification comes in with a beep or a ding or a buzz. No wonder it starts to feel like we're in an emotional pinball machine.

When I was a kid, my father had a beeper. (In the '70s, you pretty much had a beeper only if you were a doctor or a drug dealer.) And when it went off when we were in public, like in a movie theater, it was like the Red Sea parting, with people getting up and my father saying, "Excuse me, pardon me," as the whole family trailed behind him as he headed to the emergency room, where he would save a life. That's a good reason to have a device that will get you up and out of a theater. Think about how many times we get up from being where we are because of a ping that is not urgent in any way.

As a culture we are divided about this. Some of us seem to believe that technology is going to solve every problem; others believe that it will destroy civilization. I fall somewhere in the middle. Technology is wonderful! And also terrible. And both and neither, just like the people who use it.

Taking time away from technology is a tool that lets us use technology sanely. Living 24/6 does not require you to go completely off-grid, because the grid can be pretty great. Instead, it offers a way to go off once a week, and use that time to be, reflect, connect, and rethink how you want to dial up the good, dial down the bad, and create an equilibrium that lets you have the best of both worlds: the joy of tech and the joy of unplugging. Each week you get to recalibrate.

My love of technology began in the '80s with the Apple IIe and the Macintosh, and the scratchy dial-up sound of my modem, which could only connect with the library. This was before the Web existed, when you had a Rolodex instead of LinkedIn, framed photos instead of Instagram, an address book instead of Facebook, and your phone was a heavyweight object the size of a bowling ball, operated by something resembling a fidget spinner. In 1987, a high school classmate and I co-wrote a proposal called "Uniting Nations in Telecommunications and Software" (UNITAS). It was about the potential of computers to connect students across different countries, to focus on what unites us instead of what divides us.

The UNITAS proposal led me to a student ambassador program that brought high school seniors to the USSR. When I arrived in the Soviet Union in 1988, I was listening to Sting sing the lyrics "I hope the Russians love their children too" on repeat on my Sony Walkman, and then-president Mikhail Gorbachev was implementing *glasnost* ("openness"). I was one of the first Americans some Russians had ever met. However, my goal of talking about how personal computers could bring greater understanding soon wound up feeling naive and overly optimistic. I was a California teenager who had a personal computer, and the Russians were waiting in bread lines. (It also feels ironic now in light of the 2016 US election hacking that I went to the Soviet Union to talk about the potential of computers to connect us instead of divide us.)

My experience in the USSR was the first tech bubble that burst for me. I then went to UC Berkeley. Despite my father's premed plans for me (he had bought me the book *The Making of a Woman Surgeon* on four separate occasions), I was drawn to film, which I saw as a way to make change in the world. And though there were many arguments with my father about this career choice, I decided I would be a filmmaker. It was my first rebellious act.

As with many rebellions, funding was an issue.

I ran right out of money on my first feature narrative film. Afterward, I climbed out of debt working in the nascent tech industry (very nascent: I worked on CD-ROMs). Then someone showed me this new thing called "the Web." That infrastructure for connecting all the personal computers—connecting everyone's ideas and interests, connecting people—was here!

I moved back to San Francisco, the epicenter for this new medium. I began working for *The Web* magazine and, in 1996, was given the opportunity to create the Webby Awards. I knew the medium was going to change the world, change culture, and I wanted to help shape that, honoring the best of the Web and the best of the people behind it.

The Webbys grew quickly. We soon founded the judging body, the International Academy of Digital Arts and Sciences. PricewaterhouseCoopers officiated. It was an electrifying feeling, working hard with my team to make tech and the Web accessible to popular culture. I'll never forget when the young Sergey Brin and Larry Page, founders of a new site called Google, rollerbladed onto the stage in capes to receive their first award. Or when the *New York Times* deemed the Webbys the "Oscars of the Web," or the ultimate pop-culture moment, when the Webbys became a question on *Jeopardy!*

Being under thirty and working on the Web in San Francisco felt like being in the center of the zeitgeist. On the literal edge of the country, San Francisco has been on the cutting edge of so many cultural movements, from the beats in the 1940s and '50s, to free speech in the '60s, to gay rights in the '70s. Again in the '90s, it was hard to miss the sense that there was something new and important in the air.

I was intoxicated by the possibility of the Web as a democtratic and decentralized new way to erase boundaries, connect, create, and communicate. But the big lesson that we didn't yet know then, one I feel deeply now, is that connecting broadly is meaningless unless we also connect deeply.

I've always subscribed to Marshall McLuhan's view that technology is an extension of us. It's an expression of the problems we need to solve, our deepest dreams, and our need for connection. When we needed to see farther, we invented the telescope. When we wanted to extend our reach across the world, we invented telephones. Later, we created the Internet to connect and collaborate with minds all over the world. Smartphones are the latest extensions of our brains, now literally in our hands.

It's important to remember that technology is not this alien thing that renders us powerless. We sometimes forget that *we* created this; *we* have power over *it*. And while you may not have actually invented the iPhone, or the laptop, or the Internet itself, you do have a degree of control over how you use it. All technology is, after all, is a tool that extends our capabilities.

Of course, tools can damage us when they're not used thoughtfully. People have been wringing their hands over the latest new invention since the wheel rolled into view. When writing came along, Plato warned that it would end the oral tradition that relied on memory. It did, but much was gained—namely all of ancient culture and science, which only endured because written words lasted longer than spoken ones. When the printing press made books widely available, Parisians worried that the new fad, "the book," would destroy their bustling cafe culture, as people sat and read silently instead of discussing and talking. And when TV came along, people worried it would kill books. These were huge developments, and they all changed the world. They've brought some bad things with them, but they've brought a lot of good as well. Which is why it's important to discuss, debate, and figure out what we want to keep and what we want to weed out.

I spent the first part of my career trying to get people connected online. Now I'm focused on this question: How do you get people offline regularly to live a good life? What do we need to change in the tech industry to create a healthier environment for all of us?

My mother, a psychologist, always tells me life is all about process. Each generation's task is finding the parts of society that are good and leaving behind what's harmful. The digital revolution has brought enormous changes and more are coming. Living 24/6 is a way to stay grounded as we grow and adapt to this enormous shift and create the mental space to see where we need to go.

The joy of tech is that it lets you do things very fast. You can get so many things done.

But there is value in slowing it all down, too. It's satisfying and exhilarating to live in this network of tech that allows immediacy, but we also need to remember the benefits of working slowly and consciously. As Daniel Kahneman explored in *Thinking, Fast and Slow*, our minds work in both gears. We need both to build the life we want. Now I run toward my day without screens each week. I rush in order to s l o w d o w n—switching gears, going farther.

5

The Infinite Loops of Addiction

For a brief (and regrettable) period in the '90s, I was a smoker. I remember being hugged by my father and him pulling back from me in disgust, saying I smelled like an ashtray.

I finally decided I wanted to quit shortly after getting married. In true West Coast fashion, I made an appointment with a hypnotist, Dr. Jonathan Gray. It was spring of 1999, a week before the Webby Awards. I walked in with a pack of Marlboro Lights in each hand, and as I sat down, I said, "I should really just cancel this appointment. This is the worst time to try to do this."

Dr. Gray took a deep breath. "Well, you may as well try it. You already paid for the session. It will only take thirty minutes, and it either works for you or it doesn't."

I realized he was right, and I resigned myself to trying hypnosis, as skeptical and stressed as I was.

Soon, his voice began to wash over me.

"You are feeling deeply relaxed. You are going deeper, deeper, deeper into relaxation."

He spoke in a very specific rhythm. It was as if we were galloping into a meadow and then descending down a deep well, out of my body and into my soul.

"Your arms are relaxed; your hands are relaxed."

My hands unclenched the cigarette packs and they fell to the ground.

"Your back is relaxed, your thighs are relaxed, but your sphincter"—he paused dramatically and said assertively—"keep that tight." (I've had a lot of good laughs about that since. He must have had a bad experience where someone really just let go.)

I was conscious and very alert. I could hear everything he said, but I couldn't move. "Smoking is bad for you. You know that. You don't want to continue to do something that you know is bad for you."

It was as if he'd opened up my head and was speaking directly to my brain, like he had a direct phone line to my subconscious, speaking truth to neurons without any interference from me.

Then he said, "One, two, three," and closed my head back up like he was capping a tube.

Boom. Just like that, I was back in the room. I was clear. I felt very present, the same yet different.

I haven't smoked a cigarette since. It has been over twenty years, and I'm not sure exactly why this was so effective—after all, he was just telling me things I already knew. But sometimes a message sinks in only when we're open to it. The hypnosis made me perfectly receptive, and I never smoked again.

Like Dr. Gray, I'm telling you things you already know. Staring at a screen instead of the people you are talking to isn't a good way to communicate. We are distracted too much. We get lost in the vortex. Even as a culture we know it's bad for our minds, our relationships, our quality of life and society.

So I am hoping that these words will also speak directly to your brain, opening your head and heart to what you know to be true. You spend too much time on screens. It's not making your life better, and you're ready to make a change.

And then there are the things we don't really know yet. Scientifically, we don't really know what all that screen time is doing to us—to our brains, our bodies, our relationships. Research is starting to suggest it's actually rewiring our brains and possibly changing us at a cellular level. Studies show it's making us less compassionate and shortening our attention spans. Nicholas Carr provoked the tech industry by raising some of these concerns in his 2010 book *The Shallows*, and the evidence is mounting.

We used to need to make a conscious effort to plug in; now we need to make a conscious effort to unplug. According to a recent Nielsen study, the average time an American adult spends staring at a screen is seventy-four hours a week—more than we spend sleeping, eating, and having sex, combined—and the majority of it is stressful.[8] A recent study by the tech company Asurion found that the average American checks his or her phone eighty times a day. That amounts to once every twelve minutes during waking hours. According to a survey by Accel and Qualtrics, millennials check almost twice that—150 times daily.

These are new tools, toys, appendages, and we are still in the phase of unlimited, unfiltered use, which may be why technology reminds me of smoking.

———

A recent study by public health researchers Holly B. Shakya and Nicholas A. Christakis found "both liking others' content and clicking links significantly predicted a subsequent reduction in self-reported physical health, mental health, and life satisfaction," leading the authors to conclude that "the nature and quality of this sort of connection is no substitute for the real world interaction we need for a healthy life."[9]

I remember smoking a cigarette and thinking, *I can't wait to have a cigarette*, and then realized I was *smoking a cigarette*. It now reminds me of hitting the refresh button on your phone over and over, treating it not like a communication device but a slot machine.

This is exactly what slot machines, cigarettes, and screens are *engineered* to do by design. Addicting us is the whole point.

Fifty years ago, people turned to cigarettes at the exact times we now turn to our phones: waiting, standing in line, when feeling anxious or bored, first thing in the morning with a cup of coffee, last thing at night, after sex (I've also heard of people checking a text *during* sex . . . the horror). Perhaps the big difference between smartphones and cigarettes is that usually you could start a conversation with someone by asking for a light (legendary romances have begun with this very question), as opposed to the group parallel play we all seem to do today: head down, no connection with the person next to you.

Not too long ago, you could smoke in grocery stores and movie theaters, on planes, in hospitals, and even in elementary schools. The fact that smoking was so common made it harder to see how dangerous it was. As physician and author Siddhartha Mukherjee documents in his history of cancer, *The Emperor of All Maladies*, at the time, blaming cancer on smoking was like blaming the disease on, say, sitting. *Everyone* did it. How could something everyone did be so hazardous to your health?

This actually gives me hope. In my twenties, it seemed like everyone smoked. Thanks to a combination of health campaigns, laws, and cultural shifts, it's much more rare today. That was a huge behavioral change in society, so I can imagine how the same huge shift could be possible with tech use. Even if it seems unthinkable now, a similar one for screens is attainable—and necessary.

I'm not saying smartphones are giving us cancer. But I do think unchecked use of anything—be it cigarettes, cell phones, or cinnamon buns—is probably not great for us.

Like smoking, apps, media, games, and websites are *designed* to be addictive. This is true even on a neurological level. In an interview, Sean Parker, the founding president of Facebook, admitted that the company consciously set out to hook people. Tech engineer Aza Raskin, who is a cofounder of the Center for Humane Technology, explains: "Behind every screen on your phone, there are . . . a thousand engineers that have worked on this thing to try to make it maximally addicting."

And it's very effective. As Dr. Michael Rich, who runs the Clinic for Interactive Media and Internet Disorders (CIMAID) and the Center on Media and Child Health (CMCH) at Boston Children's Hospital, writes: "Our clinical experience and research have shown that it is not a specific device or activity that is problematic, it is the interactivity that attracts them, keeps them engaged, and immerses them to the point where they lose track of time and place."

Screens are also incredibly distracting. A recent study showed that just having your phone nearby—even if it's switched off—makes you less attentive.[10] When Ken is teaching at UC Berkeley, he asks his students who insist on taking notes on their laptops (which can be less effective for comprehension than taking notes by hand) to sit in a separate area. He knows that even if you don't bring a laptop to class, if the person in front of you does, you'll retain less of the lecture.

Studies have demonstrated that screens distract everyone in the room, even those who aren't using them.[11] I've started thinking about pulling out cell phones as contagious, like yawning. If one person takes their phone out, everyone else does, too. And even when the phone is facedown and off, its very presence distracts everyone around. It's today's version of being affected by secondhand smoke.

———————

Companies are incentivized to glue our eyes to the screen. It reminds me of one of my least favorite expressions I heard a lot during my decade with the Webbys: "monetizing eyeballs." My eyes hurt just thinking of someone wanting to monetize them.

Technology can be just as addictive as nicotine or heroin or any other drug; in fact, it works in some similar ways. Brain scans show that we exhibit the same compulsive brain patterns while online as we do while using drugs; clicking activates the same neural loops that narcotics do. We really are addicted to our phones.

Dr. Rich prefers a different term: "The issue I have with calling our compulsion to be online 'addictive' is it assumes you can abstain from it, like alcohol or nicotine." But technology, like food, is something most of us can't avoid, which is why Dr. Rich thinks of tech overuse in terms of binge eating. "You have to eat, so really it's about self-regulation."

We haven't done a great job self-regulating so far. The World Health Organization recently added "Gaming Disorder," which has become particularly widespread in Korea, to its International Classification of Diseases. It's becoming such a problem that there are now rehab clinics specializing in treating it.

This is especially alarming when we're talking about children and adolescents, whose brains are even more malleable and susceptible. They're establishing the neural patterns that will be with them their whole lives.

No wonder so many technology pioneers, like Steve Jobs and Bill Gates, strictly limited their kids' screen use. Younger tech titans, who've just started having kids, already seem to be following suit. (Makes you think of the drug dealers' rule of never getting high on their own supply.)

In developed countries, now that Internet connectivity is cheap and common, it's the *less* privileged who will rely on screens, because the rich don't have to and know the harm they can cause. Schools in lower-income areas with poor teacher-student ratios will increasingly rely on tablets while better-off students get more human attention both in and out of the classroom, and inequalities will only grow.

Fortunately, we are starting to see policy changes. Some individual schools are banning smartphones in classrooms, and legislation is being introduced, both here and abroad, to keep them out of schools altogether.

I'm not calling for draconian limits for kids and adults alike. But I do think we need to think seriously about what sensible screen use would look like, and we need public discussion of pros and cons, especially where kids are involved. We should expect pushback from tech companies. And we should push forward nonetheless.

This means instituting some guidelines. Thanks to Wi-Fi,

smartphones, and streaming content, unless the adults in their lives set some limits, kids can be on screens almost anywhere, with access to anything and everything, at any time.

———————

Before he put me under, Dr. Gray told me my problem was that I'd gotten so used to the action of holding a cigarette and bringing it to my lips that I couldn't imagine not doing it. I needed to disrupt my muscle memory. We don't think of screen use as being much of a workout, but there's lots of muscle memory involved there, too. Tech Shabbat helps break that. It gives you a chance to interrupt the muscle memory loop of reaching for your phone.

Living 24/6 can help prevent digital addictions from forming and can help break them when they do. It's not a detox that you do once, or occasionally, and then go back to the way it was before. It's not a digital diet, trimming on-screen minutes here and there. That's a start, but for real change I recommend more: a once-a-week lifestyle change whose effects ripple out all week long.

It's also not a twelve-step recovery program, but it does take accountability, and it will help you gain serenity, peace, and control. And, importantly, it's not about going cold turkey. I'm in no way suggesting that technology is bad and that we should quit it altogether. It's about balance. The phone itself has become, essentially, our higher power. The solution to our powerlessness, ironically, is to unplug.

Living 24/6 is a way to replenish social, mental, and emotional nourishment. It's a commitment to health and happiness that evolves and deepens over time.

If you're reading this, you might be in the same situation as I was when I walked into Dr. Gray's office. You know you're addicted, and you know you need help. You've already paid for the session, and you've got nothing to lose from trying this. So go ahead and see what happens. Begin by admitting you're on screens too much, your family is on screens too much, your coworkers are on screens too much, and it's time to take a step back. Knowing how we respond to stimuli is a good place to start.

6

Algorithms and Animal Instincts

We are animals. We may have language, morality, fancy accessories, and opposable thumbs, but at heart, we're still animals who rely on instincts. We call these instincts "emotions" or "desires," and they're extremely useful. They help us navigate a complicated world. But sometimes these emotion-instincts can be less than noble, especially where technology is involved. Though it took some high-minded human engineering to build the Web, it's not our high-mindedness the Web appeals to. More often, it speaks to our untamed nature.

We have created an online world that's designed to tempt us, prod us (are you sure you don't want to buy those boots you just spent two minutes looking at?), make us jealous (look at how much more fun they are having than you!), scare us (all jobs will be automated in ten years), distract us from the truth (fake news), prevent us from thinking of the bigger picture (text, ping, buzz), take away our power (look down, not up), and generally make us want more, more, more to distract us from acknowledging what we are really feeling. Digital culture has amplified the beast within.

The digital world manufactures, then satisfies, false needs (for "likes," retweets, and, yes, boots). And unless we consciously detach, we'll just keep clicking. We're constantly refreshing, seeking new texts, new posts, new products, new news. We're never satiated.

Websites, smartphones, and apps know our emotional buttons, and they are pushing them all the time. Like my mother says about family: they know where all our buttons are, because they installed them. With technology—which involves pushing, or tapping, literal buttons—this is even more true. We have created this system to track and push and prod and nudge us into buying, trusting, and clicking, accepting every cookie we're offered. It's only gotten worse as the Web has become more of a monolith. When it changed from a decentralized network to a behemoth centralized through a few corporations wanting to monetize every moment by playing to our animal nature, the Web really got beastly.

The people very close to us used to be the only ones who could read our minds. Now we've given corporations all the data they need to know our every thought. We've willingly cooperated from the beginning, sharing the information that let them install the buttons in the first place. We exchanged our privacy for free content, only to learn that it wasn't free in any sense of the word. We're only beginning to comprehend the far-reaching ramifications.

We need to push back.

The good news is that we can do a lot to change our behavior. Yes, the outside forces of the world will constantly tempt us to be animals, with sexy billboards, violent media, sugar everywhere, and new tech toys, but we have the agency to say no. The more we resist, the more we can strengthen the "resistance" part of the brain.

The human brain is constantly developing. Everything you do and experience is reshaping connections in your brain, strengthening some connections while weakening or pruning others. This also holds true for your online life: every link you follow, every post you read, every comment you make, is shaping the wiring of your brain.

The human brain evolved to respond to stimulation. Which means that we are in a pervasive battle with our animal instincts (eat, vape, screw, screen), while doing all we can to tame the beast (read, learn, think, practice). So, while we all need to take an unflinching look at the world we have created and all of our own vices, there are also strategies that can help us regain power over ourselves and our behavior.

One of the central quotes in a film I made called *The Science of Character* gets attributed to many different great thinkers. You know it's good when (supposedly) Ralph Waldo Emerson, Lao Tzu, and Buddha all said it: "Watch your thoughts, for they become words; watch your words, for they become actions; watch your actions, for they become habits; watch your habits, for they become character; watch your character, for it becomes destiny."

The best part about this quote is that after digging through the infinite layers of the Internet, I found that it was actually said by someone named Frank Outlaw. I relished thinking for a moment that this person who was perhaps an *outlaw* would stop and ponder this series of thoughts before he robbed a bank. Then I clicked further and found he was the owner of a chain of Southern grocery stores.

Intentionally or not, Frank Outlaw described the functions

of your prefrontal cortex. Evolutionarily speaking, the prefrontal cortex is more recent than the amygdala, which is sometimes called the reptilian part of the brain.

The prefrontal cortex is the part of your brain that literally thinks things through and lets you make good long-term decisions. It's the control panel, overseeing what's known as "executive functioning," or your thoughts and actions. Neuroscientist Adele Diamond calls these executive function skills "self-regulations." They're the skills that allow us to focus our attention, remember lists, and juggle multiple tasks. They give us the ability to filter, prioritize, and control impulses. And the way to strengthen that filter is as simple as taking a moment, focusing your attention, and asking yourself: *Is what I'm about to do a reflection of who I am? And who I want to be?* It turns out taking a moment, a beat before acting impulsively, is a big part of building one's character.

Scientific research on character development and the ability to build different character strengths (like empathy, self-control, and grit) backs up what great thinkers have been saying since the beginning of civilization. Buddha said (for real this time): "Improve your character through mindful striving. Or let your character worsen through negligence and obliviousness." Aristotle said, "Good character is the indispensable condition and chief determinant of happiness, itself the goal of all human doing." In 1726, Benjamin Franklin made a list of the thirteen virtues he thought were essential to good character and designed a daily chart to help track how well he exercised them. A couple of centuries later, early childhood education pioneer Maria Montessori would observe, "Character education is just as important to education as reading, math, and science."

These iconic thinkers were all focused on developing the best aspects of ourselves. When the field of psychology originated, in the nineteenth century, it did the opposite: it focused primarily on the things that are wrong with us. In 1990, two psychologists, Martin Seligman and Christopher Peterson, decided to flip the script. In many ways, they returned to the early philosophers' approach. Instead of focusing on what's wrong with us, they started asking, "What's right with us? What are your positive attributes and how can you strengthen them?" They came up with twenty-four character strengths that are valued throughout history and across cultures, including gratitude, bravery, kindness, optimism, leadership, and humility.

Seligman and Peterson helped us see that each person is a unique combination of these different strengths. Some, called "signature strengths," come naturally to us. Others we need to develop. But the good news is, we can. Their studies suggested that all the strengths can be cultivated, and doing so leads to a happier, more fulfilling, and more meaningful life. This was the beginning of the "positive psychology" movement, social-emotional learning, and a resurgence of interest in character education.

The body of research around character development and positive psychology has grown substantially since then. It's a happy coincidence that the rise of this field coincided with the rise of the Web, because it provides so many useful tools for controlling the animal impulses the Web appeals to. The Web plays to our weaknesses, not our strengths.

One of these tools is the belief that we're capable of positive and healthy change. At Stanford in 2006, psychologist Carol Dweck proposed the theory that people either have a fixed mind-set or a growth mind-set. A fixed mind-set is the belief that we're born with certain abilities, intelligence, and talents, and we're stuck with them. A growth mind-set is believing, *I can change. If I set my mind to it, I can improve.* This has become a cornerstone of social-emotional learning and character education.

Another one of my favorite thinkers on this subject is the psychologist Angela Duckworth, renowned for many things including introducing the character strength "grit" into the public discourse. At the University of Pennsylvania, she has done important research around practice, concluding that it's all about quality over quantity. Ten minutes of quality, devoted practice yields more than an hour of distracted efforts.

When our family first started unplugging there were things to figure out, as we did this new practice each week. But over time, not only did it become easier, we began to crave it as a way to stay sane and healthy. This is the growth mind-set at work. Tech Shabbat gives us time to foster the best aspects of our family and ourselves and to strengthen our ability to detach from the animal instinct network known as the Web.

Going screen-free weekly has made it easier to unplug happily and regularly. It's also exercised many character strengths. Research shows that one of the biggest barriers to developing character strengths is having the time. Just like building any other muscle or skill, you need to make room in your schedule for it. The day without screens is our time, set aside from everything else, to focus on developing our character. And like any workout plan, if we gave it up, we'd fall out of shape.

A lot of what 24/6 living entails is self-control and establishing a habit or a practice. "Practice," in both its meanings, is the operative word here. You become skilled at any work—carpentry, music, or gardening—by practicing. Tech Shabbat gives you the opportunity to practice whatever it is you want to get better at, even if it's just being.

So what, exactly, are we practicing when we practice unplugging? We're developing character strengths as well as practical skills. This, too, is a very old thing. The idea that we should work on ourselves is ancient and universal—emphasis on *universal*. We do this not in a self-centered way, but so we can contribute more to our community and the world at large.

Rabbi Israel Salanter, who is considered the founder of the Mussar movement (Jewish ideas around character development, ethics, and practice), said: "At first I tried to change the world and failed. Then I tried to change my city and failed. Then I tried to change my family and failed. Finally, I tried to change myself and then I was able to change the world."

So . . . what do you want to work on? Everyone's work is unique.

For me, one of my struggles is with my own impatience. And let's just say that being constantly on and available 24/7 didn't help the situation. I felt—and I *saw*—myself becoming more stressed and less calm. I've found unplugging to be one of the ways I practice patience. I can't just search for an answer or reach someone that very second. I have to slow down and operate at a different speed. Which has also helped me practice being calmer—not all the time, as my family can attest, but it strengthens that muscle in me.

The effects of such practice continue to work the rest of the week. When I feel impatience or frustration coming, I try to remember that turning off screens helps, so I turn off my phone. When I'm waiting in line or stuck in traffic, I try to embrace that time. I daydream. I sit in silence. I process.

It doesn't always work (sometimes that Twitter icon calls my name and I just have to click on it), but I try. Over the years, exercising control over the on and off switch has taught me that I really can dial it up . . . or dial it down.

Which brings us back to the prefrontal cortex, the part of the brain that plans for a better future. The depictions of the future we're used to seeing—the movie trailers promising Armageddon or politicians manipulating us with scare tactics—drive us by fear. They provoke our amygdala, the part of the reptilian brain that responds to fear, the anxious part of the brain. But when we let the prefrontal cortex take over, our vision of the future is driven instead by possibility and practicality, by a desire for the best outcome and a strategy for achieving it.

Thank goodness for opposable thumbs. Because while we are animals at heart, we also have the ability to move the dial in the right direction, to practice and practice the things we want to work on until they become second nature. So here's to knowing all the strategies and tools to tame the animal within us all.

PART III:
MAKING 24/6 HAPPEN

7

Everything You Need

Okay, you're ready to try this. Or are at least really intrigued. In this chapter I'll walk you through the basics of Tech Shabbat and 24/6 living.

Planning for your first Tech Shabbat is a little like planning a day trip to the '70s or '80s. Fifty years ago, when people were predicting what life would look like in the future, they talked about space suits and teleportation. I doubt anyone imagined we'd be culturing our own pickles and making macramé wall hangings. But here we are, and I think this desire to return to analog items makes sense. When time is your greatest luxury, the things that take the most time—making things by hand—become more valuable. Tech Shabbat allows you to take a break and remember an era when spending time on things that *take* time was part of the pleasure.

Since your Tech Shabbat technology will date to the disco era, that means your phone is on the wall and stuck there. If you don't have your landline anymore, it's time to get it back. Besides being useful when you lose your cell phone—not to mention in other *actual* emergencies—a landline can be very handy on Tech Shabbat. If people need to get in touch with you, if you want to call someone you miss, that's your portal to do it. The landline is limited. It has one purpose and no dazzling distractions.

While you're shopping in the past, get yourself a watch. Not an Apple Watch; just a watch. (Don't go crazy on me and get a pocket watch. We're not at the Renaissance Faire or the Steampunk Expo.)

One piece of modern machinery comes in handy as you prepare: a printer. Use it the day before your screen-free day to print out schedules, maps, and any other information you'll need. You'll also want to print a list of your most important phone numbers: family, best friends, doctors, special-occasion takeout, skunk-removal services, etc. Keep this by your landline. I also keep a shorter version in my wallet and our kids' backpacks, because it's useful in a weekday emergency, or when you drop your cell phone in the toilet in the airport on your way to another country. (Yes, that happened to me.)

You can also use your list when you are out and about on your screen-free day if you really need to contact someone. How do you do that? You find a twenty-first-century portable telephone booth—i.e., borrow someone else's cell phone. These living, breathing telephone booths (people) are everywhere.

You may also want a big pad of paper and black Sharpie pens. It's much more satisfying to write anything down with a Sharpie. This black Sharpie is for all the things you'd typically pick up your cell phone to deal with: write a to-do list, ask so-and-so about this, schedule that, etc. Your thoughts will circle around your head like a bee looking for a flower to land on. Let them land on

the paper, little blossoms of thought. There it is, in deep black letters, waiting for you on Sunday.

If you want to listen to music, get a record player (or go lo-fi
with a boom box) or verbal speaker where you don't have to look
at a screen. (More on that later.)

Now let's talk cameras. Humans have been compelled to document our lives since the days of cave paintings. It's only natural
that you'll want pictures from your screen-free days, especially
since that's usually when the best moments happen. Trust me: I
am a *document*ary filmmaker. I get it. I love to record my favorite
moments and relive them.

But I have to tell you, there is something delicious about not
being able to record something and just having to experience with
your non-monetized eyeballs, with your very being. When I'm
trying to document something to share on social media during
the week, I find I suddenly lose twenty minutes thinking about
how to best capture the moment, what filter to use, how to cap-
tion it just right. Tech Shabbat lets you let go of all that.

At the same time, pictures are pictures, and if you just have
to take one, here are some options. If you have an actual camera,
great. Even if it's digital, that's fine, as long as it's not a phone and
thus a portal to a whole other world of distractions. But if you
can't resist and you must take that picture and the only device
nearby is a smartphone, here's the way to do it: put the phone
on airplane mode, take that photo, and then put that thing away.
Don't spend time having everyone look at the photo, editing the
photo, and God forbid, sharing that photo.

Just put it away.

Now, I know what you are thinking: *I have to buy things and install a landline?* But let me ask you: How much are your sanity and sense of balance worth? New iPhones cost a thousand dollars. The shopping list below will run under $100 if you get all of those things, but you certainly don't have to. Some you probably have, some you may not want, and you can always make substitutions. Either way, don't let acquiring them stop you from trying Tech Shabbat. Go ahead and unplug, whether you've got the analog gear or not. You can always buy stuff later, when you know what you actually need.

But if you like to shop, here's your list:

Installing landline: $15 to $20 a month

Radio or record player, simple model: $40

Watch: $20

Sharpie pen: $2 (or splurge on a three-pack for $5)

CHOOSE YOUR DAY

We go screen-free from Friday night to Saturday night, because that works best for us, an updated version of the Jewish Shabbat. For others, it's Sunday. Either way, I recommend doing it on the weekend if you can, because these are traditionally non-workdays, and it helps you feel like you're part of something bigger than yourself when your screen-free time is on a rest day for people all over the world. But that's not always possible, so pick the day that fits your schedule.

I highly recommend you unplug for a full twenty-four hours. I know there are many people and articles recommending, "Don't look at your phone before bed," "Go for walks without it," "Don't have it on the table when you are eating." Yes to all of that, but you need the daylong break, too. Shabbat is a more-than-three-thousand-year-old practice for a reason: it works. After going screen-free weekly for nearly ten years, I know that the big benefits come from doing it for the entire day, every week. Some things just take time. As my friend Alan asks, "Do you want bread, or do you want dough?" You want bread. So give it all the time it needs.

SPEAKING OF DOUGH

It's really satisfying to do things old-school once a week. Every Friday, we make an "everything" challah to enjoy at Shabbat dinner that night. This yummy sweet bread has a crust like an everything bagel. We mix and knead it in the morning and let it rise all day. Our long-time-in-learning recipe for great challah is on page 199.

Making bread may not be your thing. (Although putting your hands in dough instead of on your phone feels pretty great.) You also might work long hours and not have time for a project you have to let rise during the day. That's okay. The idea is to have something extra and unique, be it food you eat only on that day, flowers on the table, or wine you drink only for special occasions— something that enhances and marks the day.

TELL PEOPLE

The next important step in prepping for your Tech Shabbat: tell your family (if there are guilt trips for not being reachable every second, just give them your landline number and invite them for dinner). Tell all your friends you'll be offline by announcing it through the plethora of communication tools available to us now—via mouth, on the book of Face and the gram of Insta, and if you are on Twitter, tweet that @#%$ out. Trust me. It helps to hold you accountable, and your friends and family will support you. They may even want to join. (Writing this book will hold me accountable for the rest of my life. I like that.)

Tell your boss and coworkers. I highly recommend framing it as, *I'll be more productive, more creative, happier, and more efficient if I go offline for twenty-four hours.*

INVITE GUESTS

Screen-free days are a great time to spend with friends, family, people who feel like family. We bond over food, and eating with others has demonstrated health benefits, like lower rates of depression. It's also fun, which is why we always invite guests for our Shabbat dinner to start our screen-free day. We often invite new people we'd like to get to know better, since we'll have time to talk without distractions.

Sometimes as we are thinking of people who we want to have over, it feels like we are creating a wish list of people we want to connect with. In addition to those closest to us, we also invite interesting new people. A couple of times a year we do what we call our "Chutzpah Shabbat." (I'll be throwing down a lot of Yiddish, but trust me, these words will come in handy.) "Chutzpah" means "boldness," so this one is all about inviting someone we barely know but deeply admire and find particularly interesting. It's an exercise in bravery. Make a list of people who inspire you, you want to know better, or you relish spending time with. Start inviting them over. People love being invited over for dinner.

I enjoy thinking about the idea, "The five people you hang

out with most, you become." It makes you want to choose wisely, and in a lot of ways, that's what our screen-free time is about. For Friday night, we think carefully about who we want to invite over. Sometimes it's more than five people, but the idea holds solid. Surround yourself with people you admire, people you can learn from, people who are there for you, and you are there for in return.

IF YOUR PARTNER ISN'T ON BOARD

If you're thinking, *My husband/wife/partner is way too addicted, they will never go for it!*, a great way into the conversation is to ask them, "Is there anything you wish we did more of?" Then plan your screen-free day around that. If they still won't join you, go ahead and do your screen-free day on your own. When they see how much you are enjoying your time of rest and recuperation, and how much happier you are the rest of the week, they may change their mind.

IF YOU LIVE BY YOURSELF

Your screen-free day is a great opportunity for either solo time or social time, depending on what you need that week. If it's the latter, going screen-free is even more fun if you can convince some friends to do it with you. (If they won't, but you still want to hang out, let friends know they'll need to reach you by landline or face-to-face visit, and encourage drop-bys.) Host a dinner party or game night. Make it a regular weekly event. Plan a picnic, go on a group hike, volunteer, take an art class—there are a lot of ways to have fun, not a cell phone in sight. In many cities, there are organizations and websites to help you find other people with similar interests. Find an updated list of organizations to connect with others to do screen-free days on 24SixLife.com.

IF YOU HAVE YOUNG CHILDREN

Young children are usually pretty easy to distract. Instead of framing the day as a loss or punishment, present it as a special treat or reward. Ask what they wish they spent more time doing as a family: Play games? Have picnics? Ride bikes? Instead of a screen-free day, call it Family Bike Day or Hide-and-Seek Saturday.

It's true that without screens, you may lose your go-to method for keeping the kids entertained when you need a break, which means more effort on your part. But kids are naturally great at entertaining themselves—if they're not distracted by screens—and they'll find things to do. If they need a little help, keep a list of ideas for activities on the refrigerator (invent a new game, put on a play, build a blanket fort, create a treasure hunt). See more ideas on page 185.

IF YOU HAVE TEENAGERS

People find it hard to believe that our teenage daughter enjoys our screen-free day. She sleeps in, eats great food, reads, and spends time with family and friends. Odessa, who is sixteen, recently told me: "I really think the Tech Shabbats have taught me to compartmentalize stress. One day a week I am forced to put homework to the side. Stressing about assignments I can do nothing about is not productive. I'm not responsible for replying to friends or checking social media. I feel recharged afterward. Tech Shabbat guards me from high school burnout."

WHAT TO DO ON THAT OCCASIONAL WEEK YOU CAN'T DO TECH SHABBAT

A handful of weekends a year, there is a conference or some work travel Ken and I can't get out of, or a big school event for the kids, where going without technology isn't feasible. Sometimes I'll move my screen-free day to Sunday, and sometimes I'll just do a short version. I don't like to skip my screen-free day unless I absolutely have no choice. But when this happens, give yourself a break—the whole point of living 24/6 is to go easier on yourself, and there's always next week.

8

Creating a Dream Day

You have everything you need. Get ready to unplug.

Below is our routine. It can be adapted to your own preferences and schedule. It's your day; make it work for you.

Friday Morning

Before I start work, Blooma and I mix the challah dough that will then rise all day. This is also a good time to send a reminder to guests with our address. We ask for any dietary restrictions, and we usually remind them we are tech-free for the night.

Friday Afternoon

After work, I try to stop by the farmers market to pick up some fresh fruit and flowers on my way home. This makes both the house and the dinner feel festive. I print or write out anything I might need for Saturday, like maps, schedules, or phone numbers. Then it's time to prepare the meal.

Friday Night

We host people pretty much every Friday night (except if work travel keeps Ken or me from being home). This may sound like a lot of effort, but it's the best part of the week for us, and by now we've got a system down that keeps the work to a minimum. You should feel free to tailor your screen-free night to your own tastes, entertaining often, occasionally, or not at all. If you're having people over, there's no need to knock yourself out, especially if you don't like to cook. You can go potluck. Good takeout served on a beautifully set table is another great option.

In our house, we make the same meal every Friday. This takes any guesswork out of what we are serving, what to buy, and who's in charge of which dish. Ken prepares roast chicken (a version of his mother's secret recipe). I'm on challah duty with the girls, salad and roasted asparagus or whatever vegetable is in season. Odessa takes care of appetizers, chopping the veggies, and putting out the hummus, olives, and cheese (always building a wall of crackers between the smelly cheese we like and the Parmesan she likes). Blooma fills the water pitchers and gets the kid "bar" ready with apple cider, special glasses, and drink umbrellas. As a final touch, Blooma carefully places cards at each setting. These cards are prompts on a subject everyone will be asked to reflect on and talk about at dinner.

Right before guests arrive, Blooma shuts down the iPad, and Odessa closes her laptop. I usually send one last tweet saying *I'll see you on the other side* with hashtags: *#TechShabbat #Unplug #Shabbat #24SixLife*. It is fun to see my feed filling with other people also shutting down. Then I close the laptop and turn off my phone. Ken is usually the last holdout, in his home office, racing to send out just one last email before the guests arrive.

Then we greet our guests, offer them drinks, and talk about life and the world as we share hummus, crackers, and salty, plump green olives. While we are kibbitzing (Yiddish for "hanging out and talking") Odessa braids the challah dough, and Blooma leads any kids who might be there in helping us paint it with egg yolk and sprinkle it with seeds before we put it in the oven. Soon, the chicken is almost done roasting and the challah is baking. The smells set the stage.

Eventually, after we've eaten too many appetizers, everything is ready and we take the challah out and wrap it up in a patterned cloth. Then we fill our plates, buffet-style. (I highly recommend this because no one has to serve everyone, which makes it a lot easier.) We sit at the table and conversations flow.

Now the key is to bring the table together. The traditional Jewish Shabbat meal begins with a series of blessings. If you're of a different faith or tradition, or none at all, do your version of a blessing, or a toast welcoming everyone to this meal and acknowledging the food, the people, the roof over your heads.

We start with the blessing over the candles. We tell people to hum along if they don't know the words. In our house it's always off-key anyway, so the more sounds to muffle that, the better. Next, we say the blessing over the wine, and finally over the challah. I love that the word "companion" literally means "to break bread with someone." We all tear a piece of the challah and pass it to someone else.

We always have our youngest, Blooma, tell everyone how the cards work. Being the youngest child myself, who had to fight for airtime at our family table, I like having her take charge of this. This is what she says: "Hello, everyone. Please first say your name, then one thing you are grateful for this week. Next, look at the card and share how it relates to your week." She shares first to get things started, and then off we go.

We used to go around the table having everyone answer up to four questions each: What are you grateful for? What was something that happened that week that you want to let go of? What was something you learned this past week? What is something you are looking forward to next week?

But no one could remember all of those. Then one of my favorite rabbis, Amichai Lau-Lavie, introduced us to "angel cards." Each small card with, yes, an angel on it, features a different quality, like "Love," "Humility," Strength," etc. Everyone goes around and says what the card means for them that week. It's amazing to see how these little cards let everyone share something big and deep. It's a small thing, a word on a card, barely a prompt or even a nudge. But it invites our guests to be vulnerable in a safe place. They don't have to share if they don't want to. But the invitation and the warmth that it contains seem to bond everyone around the table together.

After a year or so of using our own set of angel cards at the Shabbat table, I found another set of cards with unicorns and witty text explanations of the words, which seemed designed for the same purpose. (Blooma loved unicorns.) On one side, the cards have words like "Engage," "Benefit of the Doubt," and "Trust." (When Ken drew "Spontaneous," he took off his shoes, got on the table, and, avoiding the plates and lit candles, walked to the other end, much to the girls' delight and the guests' shock.) Because we share one deep, fun conversation, no one has FOMO that they are at the wrong end of the table. Everyone is in on it, adults and children alike; there is no separate kids' table or side conversations. We are all connecting together. Ken and I believe this has also given our daughters a strong voice and a place at the table.

I laugh a lot more on Friday night than the other nights of the week. It seems that when the phone is away, the laughter comes much more easily because I am more present to see the funny, and I let myself go for that wild roller-coaster, can't-breathe, on-the-floor laughter that rarely happens during the week.

Sometimes the instruments come out. Right near the table are guitars and ukuleles, drums and tambourines. Please don't imagine the Partridge family. Usually, in fact, it's a dinner guest who gets things started after a couple glasses of wine. They grab an instrument and the ruckus begins.

After the guests leave, we do a big family cleanup.

Then we read and go to sleep. It's the best sleep of the week.

Saturday Morning

Waking up on Saturday is the most wonderful thing. I've slept well, and we're not rushing out of the house. Even if the kitchen hasn't been totally cleaned up, we try to make the table a blank slate for the day, a literal tabula rasa.

Now that the kids sleep later than us (finally), Ken and I get to spend some time talking about the things we were too busy to discuss during the week (we'll often say, "Let's wait until Saturday to talk about that"). We also spend time with our journals, writing highlights from the past week. Rereading these journals later is delicious: all my best little moments from the year in one sitting. (One of my favorite quotes by French author Anaïs Nin about journaling: "We write to taste life twice, in the moment and in retrospect.")

I also may pull out an article to read, or a book or something

I have printed out the day before that I want to absorb in a more focused way.

Eventually, Blooma wakes up, and Ken brings our almost-too-big-to-be-carried daughter on his back down the stairs and gently plops her onto the couch. Our teenage daughter, Odessa, makes her way down later, and the day opens up like a flower in full bloom. Instead of the normal *we're late for school, eat your toast, did you forget your homework, don't forget to wear a jacket, let's go!* hustle of our weekday mornings, we relax into the device-free day.

Saturday Afternoon

Here are some of the things we do, just to give you some ideas for activities. Of course, you will add your own to the list. For more ideas, see pages 185–191.

Music. We play instruments and we love listening to it. Several years into our Technology Shabbat, I gave Ken an old-fashioned turntable. The kids were thrilled when music was released from the grooves of the vinyl. We fell back in love with albums, listening to songs in the order the artist wanted us to listen to them. We have a great record store in our town bursting with vinyl gems, and the kids marveled at the stacks and stacks of albums in piles, in shelves, in bins, with cover art that defined zeitgeists: David Bowie's *Diamond Dogs*, The Beatles' *Sgt. Pepper's Lonely Hearts Club Band*, Billie Holiday's *Lady Sings the Blues* . . . You can practically hear her voice just by looking at the album cover.

During the week, Spotify is like snacking. During Shabbat, albums are a narrative feast.

Cooking. We get all European and make a big lunch. Usually, this involves a recipe for something we haven't made before.

While we are cooking we may listen to NPR's *Fresh Air* or set a timer using the Amazon Echo, because to us, it's technology but it's not a screen that takes us down a path of digital distraction. Listening to media is definitely a gray area, but in this case, it enhances being together, so that works for us.

Excursions. Sometimes we go to the public library and pick out new books, or we just read at home. After some cajoling from Ken and me, we might go on a family bike ride or we do our California version of forest bathing (more on nature and neurons and the benefits of letting nature wash away your stress in Chapter 17). We pull out watercolors and paints or the glue gun (my favorite art tool), or we grab the basketball and shoot hoops at the school playground. Sometimes we do yoga. Sometimes we do nothing.

There are also some Tech Shabbats where we have activities scheduled, like soccer or basketball games and birthday parties. When that's the case, we've written out by hand or printed where we need to be so we don't have to pull our phones out. If we get lost, Ken is dispatched to quickly look at the GPS map, and then he puts the screen away.

This is not to say we spend Saturday in perfect harmony. We aren't dancing in a Matisse-like circle holding hands. There can be fights and the multitudes of harrumphs that occur when family spends time together—we are human. As Andrea J. Buchanan describes parenthood in the subtitle of her book on the subject: "Loving every (other) minute of it."

We also have errands and chores, but these are usually part of something fun we want to do: organize the art closet so we can do an art project, go to the garden store to get something to plant, or tidy the kitchen so we can have a clean space to cook. But on the whole, these days have a calmer, funnier, and more peaceful, present tone to them.

This is how my family spends our screen-free day. Take whatever ideas that work for you and leave the ones that don't. Journal. Play records. Cook. Go for walks. Talk. Visit. (If you're looking for more things to do by age, see page 185.) Or just do nothing and get a lot of sleep: as research is showing, we're not getting nearly enough. Repeat each week. The key is to fill those twenty-four hours with things you love.

PLUG BACK IN

It's traditional to end Shabbat at sunset—officially, when the glow of three stars are visible in the sky—but we end our screen-free day at five p.m. The girls are usually the first to go back online for their "double date with technology," while Ken and I get ready to go out. I sometimes want to extend the screen-free time longer. When I do jump back on, it's just to quickly check my messages and the news.

On Sunday morning, I dive back into the digital world, feeling completely refreshed with a better perspective and creative juices pumping in a way I know has only happened because of this one day off.

THE OTHER SIX DAYS

Living 24/6 isn't just about unplugging for twenty-four hours. It has the benefit of affecting how you interact with screens and technology the other 144 hours of the week. Inevitably, you become more conscious of it.

After I began doing Tech Shabbat, I noticed I was using my devices in a different, more manageable way (find more suggestions about how to do this on page 193). By unplugging completely for one day each week, I tempered my habit of turning to my phone at every possible moment. I stopped waking up to it and started my day with my journal instead. The other six days, when I'm on it too much, I catch myself: *Don't go down that rabbit hole.*

While I certainly have not achieved digital perfection, every week I get to recalibrate and remember what it's like off the screens, so the other six days I am more aware and intentional of how I use them. If life itself is a balancing act, this one day a week reminds me where the center of gravity is.

PART IV:
KEEPING TECH HUMAN

9

Exits and Entrances

Tech Shabbat is a great exit to each workweek and an entrance to something truly special. It makes me think a lot about exits and entrances in life, some profound and life-changing, some routine; some that we have no control over, some that we do. Some are rituals that define the week; some are interactions that make up our days.

While I never practiced Shabbat growing up in the '70s and '80s, my family did have several defining weekly traditions. My favorite was Sundays. The day always started with my mom and dad calling us into their bedroom with its slanted roof and bubble-dome skylights. We would all pile into the bed under its tall headboard covered with wallpaper of big mustard, white, and cobalt blue flowers, and read the funnies from the Sunday paper. Shortly after that, the whole family would meander downstairs for bagels and lox. Always, before taking his first bite, my father would thrust his finger in the air—with a little cream cheese on it—and say, in a great shtetl accent, "Tradition!"

Sunday school at our temple was not such a great part of the experience, but then we got to early Sunday evening—this was my favorite—when we would go to the movies. It was a treasured routine: first the film, then Chinese food and ice cream while we talked about the movie. For us, films were a way to explore morals, values, human relationships, truth, and the meaning of life. The cinema was our other temple, and I became a true believer in films as a way to bring people together, experience deep empathy, and provoke expansive conversations. If you follow the trail of popcorn, my desire to use film to delve into life's big questions stemmed from this weekly ritual.

In 1978, when I was eight, all the rituals went out the Peter Max–inspired stained glass windows as my parents hurtled toward divorce. The entire country was at a historic peak of divorce, and my home county of Marin, California, was at the epicenter.

Every family split up for different reasons, and the same ones. New no-fault divorce laws had spread like wildfire through the country. Women wanted to be fulfilled outside the home and be financially independent. They wanted careers (like my mother, who would go back to school to earn her PhD in psychology). Men, on the whole, weren't so sure.

In first grade, only one of my classmates' parents were divorced. By fifth grade, 1979, only one family was still intact. Our family was not that family. We were part of the explosion.

My family's divorce broke my heart in two. Not into a million pieces as you often hear tragedy can do. It broke it right down the middle, where I had to take sides, where there were lawsuits. The divorce went on for years. We went through our family's nest egg and the nest.

Every two days, I switched homes. I missed consistency. Still, a few traditions seemed to make it through the scorched earth of divorce. Every Sunday, we still went to the movies, and we still had bagels, lox, and cream cheese.

But there were people

Missing   from the table.

If I were to psychoanalyze myself—and I might; my mother's a psychologist after all—I would ask if my family's weekly ritual is a way to metaphorically rebuild the home that, like so many others, got broken in the '70s.

———————

So perhaps I was trying to bring back something I missed when Ken and I decided to celebrate our nineteenth wedding anniversary '70s-style by going to Esalen Institute, the famed retreat center jutting out from the rugged mountains over the Pacific Ocean in Big Sur. I had signed us up for the only class that still had room, which was called something to the effect of "Ecstatic Dancing Meditation." We found ourselves in a yurt surrounded by the sounds of a pan flute. The instructor was urging us: "Let your bodies flow like ferns. . . ." Ken whispered, "I love you, but I'm not sure how long I can last. I'm from the East Coast. I'm too cynical for this." We started to laugh and couldn't stop. Five minutes later, we snuck out a side door and into a different workshop.

The class we ended up in was designed for couples, and the instructors made it clear that there would be no group sharing. That was a much better fit. My goal was to take at least one useful piece of wisdom or practice home from any workshop, and this one taught us how to start the day with a proper entrance. Every morning, when one of us walks down the stairs, no matter what the other one is doing—writing, sipping, scrolling, typing—we stop, get up, and walk toward each other for a long hug. Not a one-armed, half-assed hug, but a two-armed, full, smushy heart-to-heart embrace. That simple. It may sound a little corny, but it frames the day in love. We do this when the girls walk down the stairs, too.

Recently, Ken and I co-led a Tech Shabbat weekend at another retreat center with Sydney Mintz, our brilliant and very funny rabbi and good friend. Her takeaway advice was also about exits and entrances: Count to ten with your hand on the doorknob when you're about to enter a new room, to make sure you don't bring the energy or emotional baggage from the previous meeting into the next one. And *definitely* don't bring in your in-progress phone call. No one wants to be greeted with half a telephone conversation that doesn't include them: half a hello, a smiley head nod with a finger up saying *I'll just be a minute* (right), and then being subjected to one side of a conversation.

When you think about it, these everyday interactions are really what frame your relationship and set the tone for the day and the night. As author Simon Sinek has said, these in-between times are when relationships get built. They also shape all of your interactions with people, whether it is the barista, the bus driver, the flight attendant, the librarian. All these interactions are opportunities to sew something positive into the fabric of society. And I worry about how much people are now looking down at their phones as they nod and grunt their way through many of these interactions, which, when added all up, make up an enormous percentage of our lives. All that eye contact, all that connection, all those opportunities to make life better. All those entrances and exits.

What all of this is really about is attention. Where are you putting your eyes when you walk into a room? My parents often described this scenario from when I was a child: My father would come home after a day of work and sit in his worn black leather Eames recliner chair with a Sherlock Holmes–style pipe and the *San Francisco Chronicle*, happily unwinding after an intense day of surgery. At some point, I would want to talk to him, and he would maybe supply some faux-attentive sound, like a "hmm." When I could no longer stand it, I would push down the newspaper and cup his cheeks in my hands, look him in the eye, and say, "Daddy, I want your undivided attention!" This story seemed to sum me all up for my parents.

Perhaps I can also no longer stand the distracted and partial attention of society. My films, my events, and this book are my attempt to cup society by the cheeks and say, *This is an important issue; we need your undivided attention!*

How did we go from the Age of Reason to the Age of Distraction?

What we are living in today is what former tech executive and writer Linda Stone calls "continuous partial attention," where no one is really paying attention to anything (other than their phones), and we've lost sight of the important stuff, like love, truth, wisdom. We don't look; we glance. We don't read; we skim. All of which means we're actually taking in a lot less. As UCLA education professor Maryanne Wolf writes in the *Guardian*, "Skim reading is the new normal [on screens]. When the reading brain skims texts, we don't have time to grasp complexity, to understand another's feelings or to perceive beauty. We need a new literacy for the digital age."

Media theorist Howard Rheingold says, "Pay attention to what you are paying attention to." When we pay attention, it reflects our values and attitudes.

I wanted to bring this focused attention to my workplace, too. So we started defining exits and entrances there as well. On Monday, we begin an email thread where everyone lists their five priorities for the week, any questions, and any key meetings that involve other members of our team. Then on Friday, to close out the week, we return to that email thread and write an update on each thing. But here is the best part: then we do "shout-outs." It can be a general comment to the team, or to each person individually, but in essence, they're bursts of appreciation/gratitude/collective acknowledgment. It's an optional thing, but for the most part, everyone participates. So basically the last email you see from work that week is a rapid succession of appreciations. It's your goodbye.

Our screen-free day involves a whole lot of entrances and exits, hellos and goodbyes. On Friday we exit the week and enter Tech Shabbat. The exit is marked by turning off our screens, and the entrance is marked by the ritual of candles and our Shabbat meal with friends. A day later, we exit our sacred time and reenter the world of technology all over again.

Focusing on creating an official entrance and exit to the week, and to Tech Shabbat itself, has an extended effect throughout the week to make you think more intentionally about all the other entrances and exits you open and close throughout the day, with your parents, your friends, the people at your work or school, your pets, your partner, your children, and all the people you interact with as you go about your day. As the French philosopher Simone Weil said, "Attention is the rarest and purest form of generosity."

10

Eye Contact and Empathy

When I was pregnant with Odessa in 2002, Ken and I took a birth class called La Mazel Tov (yes, that's a Jewish Lamaze class). Recently, I ran into the educator who led our class, Mimi Greisman, and was jolted by not only what she said to me but also the urgency of her message: "Tiffany, I'm worried. Parents bring their phones into a one-hour parent/baby class all about nurturing and bonding with their baby, and they're on their phones the whole time. I can't persuade them to put their phones down. The babies are trying to get their parents' attention. For some kids, they just give up."

The importance of eye contact starts the moment a baby is born. In those critical first months, a baby can communicate only through nonverbal communication, primarily through sight. Researchers can gauge a preverbal child's interest in an object by timing how long they look at it.

Every moment we look into a baby's eyes, we are creating synapses in their brains with vital messages about love, safety, and communicating with other humans. Eye contact is crucial for healthy neurocognitive development, stimulating the growth of myelin that helps infant brains transmit and process information.

Without regular eye contact, children languish. Which is why it's so troubling that children are at risk of having less eye contact with parents and caregivers than perhaps any generation before. Parents are spending more *time* with their children now, but perhaps they're connecting with them less. Which isn't good for anyone.

We're raising a generation that won't look up from their phones, often following our own bad example. Kids watch what we do—and they copy it. They're missing out on something essential.

The importance of eye contact goes far, far back, and was crucial to human evolution. The evolution of the human eye, which began over five hundred million years ago, would lead to the ability to hunt, escape from predators, and create tools. Over time, eyes would prove to be our most important sensory organ, able to distinguish seven million colors, protecting us from danger, and letting us develop innovations, like the alphabet, that would help us prosper and advance. More important, they would allow us to perceive the enormous range of facial expressions that help us understand what other people are feeling. These relatively small organs help us connect and develop empathy, understanding, and other qualities that make us human.

Even when someone is speaking to you, only part of what you perceive is verbal; the rest is information you get visually from the way their face and body move. You know they're telling you something surprising if their eyebrows are raised. You know it's bad news if their brows are downcast. You may know if someone is lying by an awkward twitch. If the right person looks you in the eye, you can even fall in love. It's the eye and the brain working in tandem to decipher information, to understand and to respond.

Using our eyes to look at technological tools has its puposes— but it can come at the expense of our best tool: our eyes' ability to read and interpret faces and body language in real life.

It's not great for our relationships, and it's bad for our health as well. Among other things, having our eyes glued to our phones has resulted in a new repetitive stress injury, "text neck." Other consequences are more serious. In Honolulu, distracted pedestrians have become such a problem that in 2018 local government had to pass legislation making it illegal to look at a screen while crossing the street; too many people were getting hurt.

All that screen time is not doing a lot for our mental health, either. Recently, a good friend of mine and her husband experienced what all parents fear: their teenage daughter turned into someone they didn't recognize. Like a lot of kids, she was spending all her time on her phone, but she was using it to make the worst possible connections, seeking out the substances and company no parent wants their kids to have. When I asked my friend how she knew it was time for drastic intervention, she said, "She lost the light in her eyes. I just can't describe it any other way."

Suicide rates are higher than they have ever been among the general public, and researchers are asking if frequent social media and Internet use may be a contributing factor.[12] Doctors who spend more time interfacing with medical reporting software than talking with their patients burn out at much higher rates. Other studies show that a lack of empathy and Internet addiction are closely linked. Veterinarians warn that even *dogs* are being negatively affected by a lack of human eye contact with their owners. And finally, research psychologist Sara Konrath's three-decade study of college students found that those students are a full 40 percent less empathetic than their peers were just ten years previously, with the most dramatic changes happening after the release of the smartphone.[13]

My enthusiasm for the Web in those early days of the medium was because I saw its potential to connect people all over the world in creative new ways. I never imagined it would detach us so completely from in-person connection.

We need to get it back.

———

There's another reason face-to-face, eye-to-eye contact is important: it activates something called the parasympathetic nervous system, which is vital to keeping us healthy and alive—and also mitigates some of the problems that come with excessive screen use.

The parasympathetic nervous system is known for several rhyming functions—"feed and breed" (digestion and sexual arousal), "rest and digest" (controlling heart rate and intestinal activity), and "tend and befriend" (nurturing and maintaining relationships)—all of which help us recover from another of our body's rhyming functions: "fight or flight." This is important, because even though we rarely have to flee carnivorous beasts, our fight-or-flight response is being triggered all the time by lower-stakes dangers, many of which are delivered via screens.

Before we've even gotten out of bed, our eyes are downloading the news, which is generally a list of things to worry about. Most of us don't get much of a chance to recover during the rest of the day. As we're deluged by social media updates, some can make us feel connected to others, but many can somehow make us feel more isolated, like we're missing out. Then, at night, when we should be winding down, we're getting wound up—by staring at our screens. All of which means our fight-or-flight response is constantly being activated. Fortunately, the parasympathetic nervous system can temper that. So how do we turn it on? One incredibly simple way is just to get more face-to-face social contact. "Tend and befriend" activities calm our heart rates and make us feel happier and more relaxed.[14] It's an evolutionary response that kept us alive between predator panics.

We also activate the parasympathetic nervous system when we come together to do something *for* someone else. This is why we feel great when we do things that don't necessarily benefit us at all but really help others, like cooking a meal for someone. It's how we evolved: the survival of humankind has relied on this impulse.

Now we're having to learn, very quickly, how to translate this impulse through screens. Some technologies are pretty good at this. Applications like Skype and FaceTime—which allow us to actually see the person we're speaking to—let us connect in visual ways that the phone, letters, and other forms of communication don't. And that has huge value, especially for family and friends who aren't nearby. Seeing our daughters use a video call to connect to their grandmothers is a beautiful thing. While it doesn't replace being in the room together, it's the next-best thing. (I can't wait until they invent a feature that lets us really look into each other's eyes instead of slightly off because the camera and screen are not aligned. Not to mention the compulsion to check yourself out instead of looking at the other person.)

Virtual reality technologies also hold tremendous promise for increasing our connection with each other. As studies have shown, virtual reality projects that allow you to see through the eyes of someone from a different race can make you more empathetic and less prejudiced. (Roger Ross Williams's VR documentary *Traveling While Black* is a powerful example.) VR can be transformative, letting you experience something virtually firsthand, as with Stanford University Virtual Human Interaction Lab's project *Becoming Homeless: A Human Experience.* When we have a chance to see things from another's point of view, we see with new eyes.

As a filmmaker, my eye is often behind the camera. And while I do think we spend too much time on small screens, I know the big screen can actually strengthen empathy. I've always loved the way that films are called "movies": they "move" people, letting us experience things together, reminding us of our common humanity, as we laugh, cry, sigh, and clap together. It's a chance to truly walk in someone else's shoes for ninety minutes.

———————

When my father was nearing the end of his life, he told the people closest to him—his three kids; my stepmother, Ina; and his best friend, Freddie—that he had something very important to tell us. His brain cancer was in the Broca area of the brain, which affects speech, but the part of the brain associated with comprehension (Wernicke's area) was still going strong. We all gathered around his bed, leaning into him, like a sail on a windy day dipping closer to the ocean, to hear him . . . and then . . .

He lost his ability to speak.

He was trapped with that beautiful brain and eye connection, with no words coming out, unable to move. His body was shutting down; he had only his eye contact left. This huge longing to keep the eye contact going was deep, complex, and filled with so many layers. We stayed in that emotional magnetic pull for hours, until he died.

———————

Eye contact is the first and last form of communication we have. It's fundamental. And I worry we're losing it.

Tech Shabbat is our way of protecting it. Nothing is more effective for increasing empathy than in-person, face-to-face eye contact. We look up. And open our eyes.

11

Taming Social Media

Like a lot of people, I wrestle with the pros and cons of social media. The desire to reach out and feel connected is a fundamental aspect of our species. The human brain evolved to seek out human contact. It's no surprise, then, that the need to be tagged, tweeted, and liked stems on some level from this very primal feeling of wanting to be loved, valued, and seen. It's the two-year-old at the beach, waddling toward their parents, squealing, "Look at me!" That's basically what social media is.

The medium is new, but the desire is not. There is a term familiar to Leonard Cohen fans and readers of Genesis: "Hineni," which means "Here I am." It's a profound declaration of self. But the documentation of ourselves in front of every sunset, before eating a plate of caramelized brussels sprouts, every time we walk over the Brooklyn Bridge or go to a concert, is a shallow echo. *Here I am* becomes *Look at me* becomes *Like and subscribe*. There are now almost too many ways to feel connected, to be "seen," at the expense of just "being" with one another.

Humans are hardwired to be social creatures. But this ancient, innate impulse is now being translated through this new way of being social—through social *media*—which can warp things.

My mother, with her perspective as a psychologist, says, "Success distances you from people, and vulnerabilities bring you closer." Too many social media feeds seem to be attempts to show just the successes, not the vulnerabilities, only creating more distance. It seems to me that those people who only show a perfect version of their life are usually the ones trying to hide their vulnerabilities or pain the most.

Let's remember that the other meaning of "screen" is "filter." All the social media on our screens is filtered—sometimes literally, sometimes figuratively. It's always, in some way, distorted, edited, reshaped.

All of which can result in misperceptions. We know that experience of getting an email or a text and taking offense, but then when we actually hear the words from the person, face-to-face, with body language and eye contact and all the other ways we communicate, we realize that we just interpreted them incorrectly. While emojis are an attempt to rectify this problem, not all people use them, and our infinitely subtle facial expressions really cannot be conveyed by a handful of cartoon faces. Then there's the other side: when people think that just because there's no face attached their words, they can be more cruel. There are a lot of ugly examples; just see the comments section of almost any website. Forgetting they're interacting with a person, people sometimes act less than human.

The speed of social media can also be a drawback. "Deepfake" videos—which are digitally altered to make something that never happened look very real—and violent user-posted footage can race around the world and do real harm before they're taken down, if they're taken down at all. We also post before we truly have time to think. Others pile on before they have all the details or context. Which can result in the awful ritual of social media public shaming, sometimes deserved, sometimes not, in which someone's whole life can be ruined in a matter of hours. The nuance and understanding that time and distance provide are missing from social media entirely. There is no doubt that a lot of desire to check in on social media is to feel less alone.

Sometimes, however, social media is a lifeline. Social media can help us feel less isolated, connecting us with people with similar interests, viewpoints, and identities. The Internet has met this need in unprecedented ways, and it's been unbelievably helpful for a huge range of populations: people dealing with physical or mental health problems, LGBTQ people looking for community or resources, and people who gain strength and reassurance from other members of their groups. It helps people feel less lonely, especially important for elderly people who may have trouble getting out and around.

Yet the ongoing paradox is that it can also make us feel left out and disconnected. And although it's not face-to-face, social media is still social. It lets you stay in touch. You can see your friends' kids grow up, even when they live across the country or in a different part of the world. When something significant happens—an eclipse, or the death of someone loved and admired in society—everyone can use the same hashtag to unite a conversation around it. On your birthday, you can feel bursts of love in a multitude of ways online. There are moments when what someone shares is so beautiful, deep, or raw that it brings me to tears. Social media lets my film studio host global conversations on subjects like character or gender equality or healthy screen use. Groups around the globe host their own unique events that day, and we link them all together with a livestream and unified hashtags. On any given day, I can search a hashtag to see all the different perspectives on it unfiltered. These are times when social media shines.

That's also why I love Twitter. I follow a diverse group of people and enjoy bumping into different perspectives that take me to unusual places. I read, reshare links, watch, and retweet, resulting in a very exciting, fast combustion of ideas, which has even resulted in real-life friendships and collaborators.

Social media offers a way to share ideas in a broad, scalable manner. It can facilitate the mass political organizing that has resulted in real change all over the world. If you have a project (a fund-raising pledge, an issue you care about, a book, a film), it's a great way to reach a lot of people all at once. It's quite an exciting feeling to set a project into motion online. Social media also lets you do research and development in real time, trying out new ideas and seeing the response. All of which means, unless you have a research and development lab, a printing press, a TV network, and a radio station, you'll probably need it to launch a project.

And therein lies the rub. Social media can be very useful, but as media theorist and author of *Team Human* Douglas Rushkoff has argued, with good reason, it can also be antihuman, antisociety, and antisocial, driven by commercial agendas whose priorities don't align with our own. In 2017, Tristan Harris, a former Google employee who now heads up the Center for Humane Technology, gave a TED talk titled "How a Handful of Tech Companies Control Billions of Minds Every Day." With his insider knowledge, he shared how massive investment in studying the brain was then parlayed into monetizing time and attention through options like the "Snapstreak"—a feature on Snapchat that addicts teens into having to check in every twenty-four hours with someone, or else they'll lose the streak.

In his book *Ten Arguments for Deleting Your Social Media Accounts Right Now*, computer scientist and author Jaron Lanier presents social media's many cons, including "Social media is undermining the truth," "Social media is destroying your capacity for empathy," "Social media is making you into an asshole," and "Social media hates your soul." His extreme take reveals truths we need to look at. Already, our data has been used to skew elections, spread false information, and radicalize the disaffected. It is hard for people to get their minds around the vast ramifications of this, but clearly, we need to.

Because I'm not ready to give up social media entirely, my compromise is trying to be more intentional in how I use it. I agree with MIT sociologist Sherry Turkle when she says, "I'm not anti-technology, I'm pro-conversation." In her seminal book *Alone Together*, she describes the ways technology is changing and unsettling our relationships with friends and loved ones.

Like Turkle, Lanier, and Rushkoff, I'm unsettled by these changes, too, and appreciate their viewpoints, which focus on finding ways to make tech work for us rather than the other way around. Because even though I grapple regularly with all of these perspectives like an ever-turning Rubik's Cube, I do think social media can be beneficial. My "opticism" (what Ken and I call our viewpoint, as in optimism + skepticism) usually tries to land on how we can use these tools in a positive way.

Social media lets us interact with people we would never encounter otherwise. And as long as we haven't curated our feeds into echo chambers, this means being exposed to diverse perspectives, which is crucial to grow as individuals and as a society.

I ultimately believe we can evolve when and how we are using these new forms of communication, continually asking ourselves questions around our use. For example, why are you using this particular social media channel? Is it for work? Is it to connect with family and friends? Is it wanting to present a version of your life to the world? Is it to experience other perspectives? Do you use all the social media channels for the same purpose? Do some serve certain purposes, while others don't?

Next: How often are you using them? If you're on the channels more than you'd like, well, there's a good place to start. Then, how quickly are you posting? Ask yourself questions before you post: How will people receive this information? What's the purpose of sharing it? And is this information best communicated face-to-face with close friends and family, on a call, via email or text, or on social media?

In my daughter's fourth-grade class, there is a lot of talk about not discussing "fun playdates" with another person in front of someone else because it makes them feel bad and left out. When does it ever feel good to hear about a playdate or party that you weren't invited to or a fabulous vacation you didn't go on? That's a lot of what's on social media. Whether it's kids, teenagers, or adults, I don't think we ever age out of feeling left out.

We need to recalibrate as each new iteration of social media arrives, because each presents advantages and challenges, and tools we can't even imagine are still to come. I was going to attempt to unpack Snapchat—which younger users turn to more than texts or email—but Odessa warned, "Mom, don't write about something you don't understand." So I asked her to dissect it, along with giving strategies about using it so it doesn't use you. Here is what she said:

"The appeal of Snapchat has moved beyond disappearing messages. Perhaps that's what drew people to it originally, but now Snapchat is like a common room. The majority of Snapchat is just communicating with friends, not publicizing yourself like on other platforms. Snapchat allows communication beyond the text; you can use your face to illustrate your point, or take quick videos to rant or explain. Snapchat is frequently disparaged because most adults don't understand its function, focusing instead on its secrecy, the vanity of its selfie-taking filters, and its infamous 'streaks.' But we just see it as the new way to communicate, like a telegram, phone call, or text."

Snapstreaks are designed to keep users online, and Odessa quickly figured out she needed parameters. She says: "I tend to go on Snapchat rather sporadically depending on my stress level and the length of my to-do list. For a while, I kept with it because I was afraid to lose connections with people. But these connections can be quite shallow, although you are communicating every day. You can have a streak with a person but not talk at all while at school. Once I let go of needing to keep up streaks, I focused on going onto Snapchat only when I wanted to, not for the sole purpose of keeping up a streak."

It's helpful to have a social media strategy no matter what age you are. I've tried a lot of different strategies, and this is what works best for me: I highly curate who I follow on some channels, and open it up wide to a lot of different perspectives on others. On Instagram, I follow only very good friends who post rarely and people who make art or design. On Facebook, I follow only family and friends who live far away, and those who post things that truly make me think. On Twitter, I'm much more in my head and not my heart. I follow a wide range of people with many different views than mine—they get me out of my bubble. I also frequently go to a website called AllSides.com that shows the headlines from the left, center, and right on big news. I try to never look at social media before I go to sleep, because those people often show up in my dreams. Be careful who you let into your head.

I finally realized I needed to turn off all notifications on my phone except for calls or texts from key family and friends. Do you really need notifications to alert you to every piece of stressful news, every like or retweet? These kinds of alerts may make us feel important, involved, and valued, but it can be even more empowering to turn them all off and choose when you go in and check. Given that it takes twenty-three minutes to regain focus after you have been interrupted, how much time do you want to lose because of social media notifications? We all want to feel connected, but it's important to be sure that it's to something that feeds instead of drains you. Last, I try to take social media breaks. Taking the occasional week off from Instagram, Twitter, and Facebook can be great for your schedule as well as your soul. This is what my weekly day off does as well. See how you feel.

On social media, we're all plants, leaning toward the sunlight we can't get enough of, seeking the warmth of likes, hearts, and retweets. But staying rooted and grounded is important. Being intentional about how you use social media and having your own strategy gives you time to process how it's affecting your life and find what you may want to change.

12

Left to Their Own Devices: Parenting with Tech

Odessa may have been one of the last students at her high school to get a smartphone. Though Ken and I (mostly) love how tech can change the world, we weren't so sure we wanted it to change our daughter. We already knew firsthand how much having smartphones had changed us in many not-so-great ways.

Today's Generation X parents are the first—and the last—generation to have lived half our lives offline. This gives us a unique perspective on connecting—and disconnecting. We're also raising the first generation of kids who will grow up entirely online. But we're not the first to shepherd our children through new technologies. When TV came along, for example, parents agonized about the effects. I grew up feasting on *The Brady Bunch*, *The Love Boat*, and *Mork & Mindy*, and that was the big concern when I was a kid: TV was going to turn my brain to mush.

Parents had reason to worry. Research showed young viewers couldn't distinguish between TV programming and ads, and the programming left a lot to be desired. In 1990, the Children's Television Act was passed, mandating educational content and limiting advertising. Reporting requirements were instituted, and more legislation followed. Parents began monitoring their children's viewing more, and we all grew up (relatively) well-adjusted and normal.

Back then, there were only a handful of channels. Now there's an infinite array of videos and games, available anywhere and anytime, subject to little oversight. TV also had physical limits: you can't drag a big TV with you into bed, into the bathroom, on a walk, into the classroom, or in your pocket for a hit of entertainment and distraction whenever you want.

Screens have become like members of the family. They sit with us at the dinner table. They go to sleep with us. We worry if we can't find them, we feel anxious when they aren't in sight, and we get upset when we leave them at home. But they make some of us wary. We're wondering how this sea change may be affecting kids, and if phones should be as regulated as TV was. What will smartphones and screens do to children's developing minds?

Potentially, a lot. Child and adolescent brains are in major growth mode, and these new technologies were simply not designed for developing brains, which are particularly vulnerable to every kind of input. Young brains are incredibly malleable. Babies are born with a hundred billion neurons—the same number adults have—but the neurons aren't all connected yet. Kids are learning to make sense of the whole world, and their brains are forming connections at breakneck speed. Those connections are created through every interaction a child has and are important because they form the architecture of the brain. So every experience a child has is creating new neural connections. This is especially true from birth to age five, when a child's brain will develop most rapidly.

Children's brains go through another period of dramatic development during adolescence. During the teenage years, the amygdala—the part of the brain that channels impulses, emotions, instincts, and aggression—is on rapid-fire. And the prefrontal cortex—which rules decision-making and critical thinking—isn't fully developed.

Teenagers lean heavily on their amygdala during this period—much more than (most) adults do. What must 24/7 connectivity do to the part of the brain in charge of emotions and impulses? How is the developing adolescent brain affected by the addictive behavioral impulses that technology provokes? Research from Common Sense Media reports that teenagers are using some form of online media *nine* hours a day. That's more than half of their waking hours.

While parents have always worried, we're definitely in new terrain. We're also now worrying that our kids are *too* risk averse. In more privileged social strata, there seems to be a trend in raising a generation that's delaying adulthood. Fewer teens are getting driver's licenses or after-school jobs. Kids are so preoccupied with their smartphones that they aren't even dating. Instead of sex, drugs, and rock 'n' roll, it's become text, vape, Snap, and scroll.

Because developing brains seem to be even more vulnerable to Internet addiction, prominent tech investors have begun urging Apple to put some safeguards in place, and Apple has started to comply, offering monitoring and time limits because the shareholders demanded it. There *is* good reason to worry. Teens who spend five or more hours a day online are twice as likely to say they're unhappy. It's particularly damaging to their attentiveness:

in a survey of teachers by the Center on Media and Child Health at Harvard's Boston Children's Hospital and the University of Alberta, 75 percent said students' ability to focus on educational tasks had decreased. Smartphone use also seems to be blunting their emotional development. A study done at UCLA showed that kids who attended a five-day screen-free outdoor camp scored much higher on empathy indicators than kids who hadn't.

Screens are also causing more family conflict. In a survey by the American Psychological Association, 58 percent of parents complained their kids were "attached" to their screens, and 48 percent said getting kids off screens was a constant battle. At the same time, however, kids will also often say their parents are constantly looking at their *own* phones, an equally important observation.

Interestingly, *no* screen time doesn't seem to be great for kids, either. Connecting does offer some benefits, though keeping that balance is hard. Research has found a happy medium. A study led by Jean M. Twenge out of San Diego State University showed that the happiest teens are the ones who spend one to two hours a day on social media. (Those of you without kids or teens are probably thinking that sounds like a lot, but remember this is out of the average nine hours most teens are online daily.)

Younger children are spending a lot of time online as well. Common Sense Media found that children ages eight to twelve spend an average of six hours online daily, and children under eight spend about fifty minutes.

These younger children are entering a world very different from the one their parents grew up in. Kids have so much access to information—many wonderful ideas, but also porn, violence, racism, misogyny—and they're learning things from dubious sources instead of from parents and grandparents or teachers. Can we really filter and shield all of that? If we think about how storytelling has been the best way to teach the next generation since we sat around ancient campfires, what kinds of stories are today's kids hearing? Who are they hearing the most from? Us, their teachers, or people online? I think ultimately our filters as parents need to be much more acute.

Common Sense Media is working to establish a filter legislatively with the KIDS Act, which would extend the protections of the 1990 Children's Television Act to all media, updating the act for the digital age. This is an important move. We also need to start thinking about what all those hours online are doing to children's developing brains. Young minds are taking in a lot more than they can process. If we hand them a screen every time they express boredom, or they start to reach for one, what are we reinforcing then? What connections are screens strengthening? What connections will they prune? We're living in an experiment in real time.

Tech Shabbat was an experiment, too, and a few years in, Ken and I could see it had real benefits for our children. They weren't nearly as attached to screens as so many of their peers were, and they became good at entertaining themselves. They came to view Tech Shabbat as a treat and not a punishment, though, as Odessa admits, it took her some time to realize that. "For my six-year-old self, it meant no more Saturday-morning cartoons or asking for my parents' phones in the interim of our fast-paced schedule," she recalls. But now our screen-free day is her favorite day of the week: "On Friday night, I do not find myself going to bed stressing about what I have to accomplish tomorrow. I sleep better than I do the rest of the week. On Saturday, the house is cocooned in an otherworldliness that comes from no digital connection with the outside world. My family is so much more with each other."

Our youngest, Blooma, who doesn't remember life before Tech Shabbat, has loved the day from the beginning. At age nine, she told us it was her favorite day because "I get to spend more time with my family. We can do arts and crafts, swim, dance, and more. So many kids don't realize how fun it can be until they start doing it."

That's not to say they aren't ready to go back to screens Saturday night. They love being both offline and online. We hoped that getting Odessa a phone wouldn't change that. Most of Odessa's classmates were given smartphones at their fifth-grade graduation in 2014, as if it were a rite of passage. Thirty-one percent of kids ages eight to ten have smartphones, and 69 percent of eleven-to-fourteen-year-olds do. We weren't ready for that, and we didn't think Odessa needed one. The issue of getting your child a smartphone is like peer pressure for adults. Everyone's doing it.

At that point, we were five years into our living 24/6 experiment, and we'd all really grown to appreciate that protected time without phones. The idea of giving Odessa unfettered access to a supercomputer disguised as a phone the other six days gave us pause.

Instead of a smartphone, we gave her a mobile flip phone for calls and texts. (I hate how flip phones are referred to as "dumb phones." Let's just call everything what it is. A flip phone is a "phone" and a "smartphone" is an "addiction machine.") We created a flip-phone contract (based on Janell Burley Hofmann's funny and astute smartphone contract, available online) with terms of use, and all three of us signed it in a ceremony at our kitchen table using an ink pen with a long pink feather attached. Very official. And that was that.

Four years later, a freshman in high school, Odessa rarely used the flip phone. It was hardly ever charged and often left at home. Ken joked that he'd consider it a miracle if Odessa picked up when he called. She explained that she just doesn't like talking on the phone. She didn't always like to be reachable. (Author and Internet law scholar Brett Frischmann says we've moved from helicopter parenting to "drone" parenting, surveilling our kids' every moment through their phones.) I used to love walking home from school by myself in the '70s for that same reason: some time to myself. I also think Odessa thought her flip phone was pretty useless because it didn't do what all her friends' smartphones did. I get that, too.

By the time Odessa was in high school, we knew we were close to the precipice. We wanted her to have what she needed to thrive. We also didn't want to do the wrong thing.

A number of events eventually made us take the plunge. She got stranded several times, once needing to borrow a phone from a mother she didn't know. She was put at a disadvantage on assignments from school because her public high school teachers assumed all kids had smartphones. Another time we couldn't reach her when she needed a ride home from a Model UN conference. She walked through the streets of San Francisco as it got colder and darker, convinced she could walk to the destination across town, because she couldn't find a cab or call a Lyft or an Uber. That one was scary. We felt that we had let her down. It was true we wanted to teach her resourcefulness and how to make do with or without technology, but we knew we couldn't hold off much longer.

While Ken was clear that now was the time to get her a smartphone, I wasn't done wrestling. Technology and sugar are two things I feel our culture audaciously pours into our kids without enough limits. There are so many other things we don't have control over. But those two, we have at least some. I have no problem going against the norm, especially when the norm has so many downsides. As parents, our job is to protect our children until they are ready to make their own decisions. We have to help them build habits that they will hopefully keep when they move out or when we are gone. (See some recommended guidelines on page 193.)

My deep gut worry was that a phone would shift Odessa's focus, as I knew it had mine. Recently, a good friend admitted that getting her ten-year-old a smartphone was the worst thing she has done as a parent. And while Ken and I have had second thoughts about our own parenting decisions, at least we were feeling like we were on the right track about holding out on the smartphone. But if fifth grade and ten years old was too early, was ninth grade and fourteen and a half the right time? Did we want to put Odessa on that digital treadmill just yet?

Even without a smartphone, Odessa was not exactly Amish. She'd had a laptop since fifth grade, and while she once used it mostly for writing, more recently there had been a lot of YouTube and binge-watching old episodes of *The West Wing*. She was on social media. Teenagers are pretty great at figuring out how to work around rules and constraints, even with just a flip phone, an iPad, and a laptop at their disposal. She MacGyvered the crap out of that situation. She was able to get in touch with people through a digital Rube Goldberg type of contraption, linking different devices that let her interact on social media and coordinate with friends without a smartphone.

But from the beginning, even with her laptop, we did have boundaries. We've always limited her screen time: thirty minutes for recreational surfing after all homework is done. Which has, of course, become increasingly hard with so much homework done online. Our daughters aren't allowed to bring screens into the bedroom except Kindles. We have a family meeting every six months to reassess and remind everyone of our family rules around tech, sugar, and chores.

When I knew we were near the end of the smartphone hold-out, we asked Odessa to write an essay about how it feels to be one of the only kids her age without a smartphone before she forgets, before her perspective changes. She said things in her essay like: "I have held too many conversations with people's foreheads." "Scrolling and talking is such a sign of disrespect." "When I am talking to someone and they are looking down, I feel as though I am talking to a portion of them and someone or something much more exciting is holding their attention. Do I not deserve their full attention?"

She says that not having a smartphone taught her how to be bored. "Not having a phone," she wrote, "has taught me how to keep myself occupied with just my imagination. Or I people-watch. Sometimes I try to think in Spanish, to carry out a conversation with myself, for as long as I can." It gets her out of her head, too: "I also am now well-versed in the ancient art of small talk due to not having a smartphone. In a socially awkward situation, I am unable to avoid it just by immersing myself in my screen, so I'm forced to make conversation, and it has taught me to appreciate these interactions."

I was writing about the situation, too. I filled my journals with my concerns:

Odessa is a very focused and thoughtful child. And yet. Will she stay that way?

Other parents would say things like: "It's inevitable." "It's the world we live in." "You don't want to leave her out socially." But even without the phone, she's in the world, she's social, and she is fine. Her laptop and borrowed phones grant her access to the garden of addictive social media delights. She is not deprived. Still, I worried that the smartphone *would* deprive her, bit by bit, of presence.

While it was once gauche to pull out your phone as you spoke to someone, it's now commonplace. While you would never put a phone on the dinner table, now people do more often than not. While we once bantered with others at the gym, bus stop, elevator, in line at the grocery store, we now stare so intently at our phones. If some mythical teacher did roll call on society right now, few could raise their hand and truthfully say, "Present."

But Ken and I knew it was time, and we knew Odessa was ready. Because, thankfully, she would always have the perspective of being without screens for one day a week for our Technology Shabbats. Hopefully, it will continue to ground her like a foundation, as it has for me and Ken.

So we finally got her a smartphone, proceeding carefully. We crossed that road together with our smartphones stuck firmly in our palms, reminding her, *Let's look both ways before we step into the future, and keep our eyes open; distractions could run us down.*

———

Soon, our youngest daughter, Blooma, will graduate fifth grade, and I'm amazed by the changes that have taken place since Odessa

did. In those five years, a lot of research has confirmed the benefits of waiting. There are many studies coming out now that speak to why we hesitated.

Smartphones and too much social media use have been linked to higher depression rates. A 2018 Vanderbilt University study is particularly alarming, showing that the number of teens treated for suicidal behavior doubled between 2008 and 2015—the exact period of growing use of smartphones for teens.

This has resulted in calls for change. At the forefront is a group called Wait Until 8th, founded in 2017, whose pledge asks families to wait until eighth grade (age fourteen) to give their kids smartphones (I now serve on its advisory board). They warn that smartphones are changing childhood: they are addictive, impair sleep, interfere with relationships, and increase the risk for anxiety, depression, and exposure to cyberbullying and sexual content. Tens of thousands of families around the country have already signed the pledge.

ScreenSense, a group of Northern California parents and teachers who provide resources for healthy tech use, makes an excellent point: We take sixteen years to transition our kids from car seats to driver's licenses, with lots of ramping up on the way to ensure they progress safely. We should do the same with smartphones, limiting kids' time and activity online until they can be trusted to use them wisely.

Of course, kids will give you pushback. Your spouse, ex-spouse, or coparent may as well. Hopefully, you can all come up with a policy that limits children's exposure to screens while allowing them to stay connected.

At Blooma's elementary school—the same school where many parents couldn't believe we didn't give our older daughter a smartphone at fifth-grade graduation five years ago—a group of parents and educators have come together to promote the Wait Until 8th pledge and advocate for simpler phones in the meantime. In March 2019, California introduced legislation to ban smartphones from schools. France has already made this nationwide law, banning phones in schools for students under fifteen in 2018. People are realizing the pendulum has swung too far.

If you've already given your child a phone, don't worry: you haven't ruined them, and there's still time to institute new guidelines for smart and responsible use. Let them know that your thoughts on tech use have changed based on new research, and that your role as a parent is to reevaluate things as they evolve. Share what you've learned, and ask for their input as well.

Society managed to survive the introduction of the alphabet, the pen, the printing press, the radio, the telephone, and the television, all of which inspired philosophical panic when they were introduced. It feels like we've hit that apex of philosophical panic in terms of smartphones and 24/7 connectivity, and that it's time to do something about it. I also believe that, like every generation before, we will figure out how to make this new technology work for us.

My father, who was fond of quoting Sophocles, used to say, "Nothing vast enters the life of mortals without a curse." Digital technology may be new, but massive cultural change isn't, and our role as parents stays the same: to do our best to guide our children through a shifting world.

13

Making Rules, Breaking Rules

I wear bright red lipstick and a hat. Always. I often get asked about the hat; the lipstick, not so much, but I'll start there. As a child, I was teased at school about having big lips. This was the era of the WASPy, thin-lipped ideal of Christie Brinkley. By the time I was a freshly minted teen, I remember telling my wise grandma Frances about the situation, thinking she would understand since it was her plump "Shlain lips" I inherited. She quickly snapped open her Lucite purse and, with her sun-spotted hands adorned in baubles of all colors, pulled out a red Chanel lipstick. She said matter-of-factly, "Darlink Tiffy, what you are teased for is one of your greatest assets. Put this on and wear it proud. It will make people pay attention to what you say, and you always have a lot to say." Done. It hasn't come off since.

The hat starts with my mother's father: Grandpa Herman. I like to think of him as the "Mayor of Malibu." He was a debonair man who looked like Humphrey Bogart, dated Hedy Lamarr, and was married and divorced many times—twice to the same woman and twice to women named Lillian.

Grandpa Herman wasn't actually the mayor of Malibu (though he had been mayor of La Quinta in Palm Springs), but in the years I visited him, he lived in and epitomized Malibu in all its sunsets-and-palm-trees, '70s faded Polaroid glamour. He was a self-made man, received a Purple Heart for being shot down when he was a pilot in WWII, and brought the technological infrastructure necessary for television to work in Palm Springs. He was a master bridge player who taught Sinatra. He was also very generous. He welcomed people of all backgrounds into his house, he challenged rules that didn't make sense to him, he lived by his own code, and he wore a black beret. I idolized him. Everyone did.

When he died, my mom gave me his beret. I wore it throughout middle school. I felt like I was wearing his perspective on my head, letting people know I had a link to this unique, colorful person. I liked the feel of a hat. When I put a hat on, I was ready. Ready. For. Anything. And ready to make things happen. That beret evolved into a fedora and an array of hats that imbued me with an extra sense of power. They also challenged gender norms . . . I liked that part, too.

When it was time for my eighth-grade graduation photo, the school rules clearly stated "no hats." This rule made no sense to me. I wasn't going to let that deter me from expressing my individuality. I was student-body president, so I started a petition to change the rule. I am wearing a hat in the school photo, and it's a portrait of the true me: someone who likes challenging the system, breaking rules that don't make sense, and creating rules that do. Like Grandpa Herman.

Humans have a unique affection for making rules and then finding a way around them. Shabbat itself may be one of the best examples. After the Talmudic rabbis list the thirty-nine distinct categories of work that are forbidden on the Sabbath, they devote a great deal of energy to finding ways around them. They pretty much have to. With that many rules, some are bound to conflict. How do you have warm food and light on Shabbat, as you're supposed to, if you can't start a fire? You create loopholes that let you observe rules you otherwise couldn't.

I'm devoted to my screen-free practice, but I'm willing to make exceptions for technologies that enhance the day (like using Alexa to set a cooking timer or listen to a podcast), and Ken sometimes makes exceptions, too. In his words:

"Some want to observe Shabbat to the letter of the law, avoiding any infractions, however minor; that's their choice. For me, Shabbat provides valuable guidelines, not a zone fenced in by barbed wire. Don't get me wrong, I appreciate the value of rules and policies and regulations, but I appreciate even more the ability to bend them. Some might counter that it's a slippery slope: make one exception and soon, anything goes. I disagree. There are many rules that allow a little slack that don't degenerate. Like speed limits and hotel checkout times. It's okay to go a little over. For me, the spirit of Shabbat is to open up space for reconnecting with family, friends, art, ideas, and nature. It's a license not to feel guilty, not to work or read email or worry about all the responsibilities I'm happy to shoulder the rest of the week."

So what's the point of making rules in the first place if you're just going to break them? Wouldn't it be better not to waste time by making rules at all? I don't think so. As philosophers Locke, Rousseau, and Hobbes argued over the centuries, we need some common rules to function. These limits are, paradoxically, what protect our freedoms. We all agree to give up some natural freedoms to live together in the relative harmony of political order.

Society is founded on these norms and guidelines: we call it the social contract. Rules and social contracts are what let us coexist as a society. If you just think of your typical day, rules are really helpful. Stopping at red lights, respecting other people's property, wearing clothes when you leave the house—these are some guidelines we all appreciate. Just picture a trip to the grocery store without commonly accepted rules: kids would be licking the produce and everyone would be cutting in line, only paying if they felt like it.

Rules can save time and mental storage space. When something's settled law, like which side of the road to drive on, you don't have to waste time or thought every time you get behind the wheel. You can devote your minutes and brain cells to matters more worthy of your brainpower.

Rules also give us something to push against and build on, and when we're creating, that can be especially useful. If someone tells you, "Write something," you'll probably reply, "I don't know what to write." But if someone says, "Write a haiku about what you ate for breakfast," you'll quickly be inspired and complete the assignment. And then, because you followed the rule, you'll reward yourself with a doughnut you know you shouldn't have. Because while we need rules, we also need to break some of them. We're human. And it's definitely what makes us different from computers. Computers operate on rules; that's essentially what coding is. But they can't *break* the rules. Humans can. Humans *have* to. And when humans break the rules or take an unexpected path, that's often when the magic happens. Getting lost can sometimes let you discover new places and connect with new people. Seems like we've lost getting lost. We're following the rules of that GPS so closely now, there's no chance we may find an interesting detour.

———————

When I started the Webby Awards in 1996, my goal was to do everything to rethink the tired model of award shows. I wanted to honor the alternative medium of the Web with an alternative awards show to match. One big variable in the show was the acceptance speeches. Cintra Wilson, our very first mistress of ceremonies at the first Webby Awards in 1997, suggested a five-word acceptance speech rule. She wore a dominatrix outfit and carried a whip for anyone who went over those five words. No one did. I thought that was a fantastic solution and instituted it going forward as our Webby Awards rule. It became the best part of the show. People got so creative, paradoxically freed up by having the constraint of just five words.

One of my favorites was when Prince came to receive a lifetime achievement award. Being a maverick with all things tech and music, he leaned into the microphone, said his five words: "Whatever you believe . . . is true," then threw down his guitar (of course he did). What an exit. I try to remember that line to conjure up empathy when I get exasperated with someone with a differing political belief than my own.

Or Al Gore, who received an award shortly after the 2000 Florida recount. His five-word speech: "Please don't recount *this* vote." The audience roared. In the twenty-plus years of the Webbys, no one has gone over the five-word limit. To this day, even though I'm working on other projects now, I still kvell (Yiddish for "feeling happy and proud") when the winners are announced and marvel at the ingenuity of the speeches and how the five-word rule is a constraint that keeps on giving.

————

Without rules and limits, freedom can be overwhelming. As Søren Kierkegaard put it: "Anxiety is the dizziness of freedom." This is especially true now when our limits are so few. We can buy anything from anywhere in the world any minute of the day. We can talk to anyone, anytime. We have infinite choices, a vast ocean of options that we can get lost sailing on.

When we unplug on Tech Shabbat, we impose limits, rules, and boundaries. It reflects one of the things Ken and I learned early on as parents: our kids will thrive with the right amount of freedom, but also with structure and limits. Turns out it wasn't just our kids who needed it. On Tech Shabbat, we build a metaphoric house for our family, Heschel's "palace in time," where we're not distracted by all the things we can read on the interweb, all the images and articles we can retweet, all the Instagram feeds we can scroll through. Imposing that structure, in turn, gives us more freedom.

The rules and limits of living 24/6 feed and reward curiosity. On our screen-free days, we're constrained in a lot of ways. When we have a question, we can't just "wonder-kill" it, i.e., Google the answer. We have to wonder. And debate. Postulate. Sometimes we even look it up in a book. The problems that can be solved with a click during the week take a little more ingenuity on Tech Shabbat. We've had to come up with creative solutions on our screen-free days, and ultimately, they've made the day more satisfying.

Of course, the limits we *don't* enforce are part of the fun of Tech Shabbat. All the things we deny ourselves during the week—

challah, sleeping in, lazy mornings, reading for pleasure, playing, art, cooking—we can enjoy without guilt.

One of the reasons we like our day with limits so much is that we know the day itself is limited. If we lived that life seven days a week, not only could we not pay our mortgage but we'd also start to get restless. It would also be pretty unhealthy. We don't want our daughters to have lazy mornings seven days a week. The fact that our Tech Shabbat is for a set twenty-four hours, every single week, makes it sacred, and makes it a ritual—a *rule*—that we look forward to every week.

In 1998, my sweet grandma Frances, who was at that point blind but just as charming, moved to San Francisco from Boca Raton, because, she said at age ninety, "I need to leave; there are too many old people here."

She was a ham and came out of her shell even more during her last year. To open the second annual Webby Awards, I wheeled her out onto the stage at the Herbst Theater in front of a boisterous sold-out audience that I thought could use her grounding presence and hard-earned wisdom. She belted out an updated version of the Bessie Smith song "A Good Man Is Hard to Find": "A good website is hard to find. You always get the other kind."

We both wore our red lipstick. We had a lot to say.

PART V:
THE SCIENCE OF
UNPLUGGING

14

Daydreaming and Creativity

I space out a lot on my one day a week without screens. Spacing out used to have such a bad connotation when I was younger. We would be reprimanded if we were daydreaming in class. But daydreaming lets you conceptualize, beta-test, make movies in your head. It lets you travel through the past, present, and future. How is that a waste of time?

Now I crave that cosmic mental trip, and I want our kids to do it more. Recently, Blooma declared she was bored during a Tech Shabbat. When I replied with my ready list of things to do (draw, cook, play basketball, pull out a puzzle, play a board game, etc.), she sighed. But then she quickly came up with an intricate treasure hunt, with clues all written in rhyme. One of my favorite sayings, wrongly attributed to Dorothy Parker, is posted on our fridge: "The cure for boredom is curiosity. There is no cure for curiosity." (Parker also gets credit, correctly, for one of my other favorite lines: "I hate writing. I love having written.")

Boredom and daydreaming are some of creativity's biggest

sources of inspiration. The science is clear: letting our minds idle can lead to big ideas and big breakthroughs.

I know my mind likes it when I take it out to wander, to think off leash. Some of my best ideas seem to come from when my mind goes on epic wandering journeys while my body is either still or busy with a mindless physical task. I get a lot of ideas doing the dishes, driving (I love an open road to think), taking a long shower, and exercising.

It's all thanks to the default mode network, the enormous system in our brains that kicks in when we're zoning out and allows us to make new connections that can lead to our most creative and insightful thoughts. (This network really is enormous: it consists of 60 to 80 percent of our brains.)

The default mode network flips on when we are "spacing out" or when our body is occupied with something else, like cleaning, bathing, or doing any physical activity. And when our brains are in that wandering mode, we imagine the future, reflect on memories, and think about other people's perspectives. There's no real structure to these thoughts—it's all stream-of-consciousness. So our minds find connections between things that we didn't see as connected before.

Recently, at cycling class, I was thinking about exits and entrances for this book. Before long, my mind cycled over to the idea that the first line of a book is the entrance, just like the first five minutes of a film is a cinematic doorway. *Then* I thought about the etiquette of entering or exiting a room when you're on the cell phone. *That* brought to mind an embarrassing "exit" I once made from a meeting when I was a young adult. I'd been planning to quit for months. Soon I was reliving the scene: The day had finally arrived, and I was in the conference room with my bosses when I blurted out, "I quit!" then went to make a dramatic exit. I had planned to slam the door, but when I went to leave, the door was locked. After a few failed attempts, I had to sheepishly walk around the table, right by the bosses in front of whom I had just quit, and out the other door (and it was a narrow conference room, so I had to say, "Excuse me," as I attempted to squeeze by them). Humiliating. Then I wondered if that would make a good opening scene of a movie or a bad sitcom. And then the lights went on and the cycling class was done.

That little ride was the default mode network. Well, it was *my* default mode network. Yours would take you somewhere else— nobody else has the combination of memories, experiences, and perspectives that you do. The paths you take through all those places are unique.

A huge part of creativity comes from letting your mind wander to make new, unusual connections. We used to spend so many more hours just zoning out, sitting in a waiting room or a subway car, staring into space. Now we have all these screens right in front of us all the time, and it's so tempting to just stare at that screen instead of letting our minds wander.

When we succumb to our screens too often, we're just spinning our wheels when we could be *going* somewhere. Because the default mode network lets us do something that's otherwise only possible in science fiction. When we let our minds wander, we can zip from the past (remembering a job I hated) to the future (imagining my next movie), all without moving from our seats (or stationary bikes). The default mode network lets us play with space and time in a tangential, meandering, incredibly complex way, and most of us think nothing of it.

So what's the difference between zoning out on our own and

zoning out on our screens? When we space out on our own, we're making our own connections and following them. But when we do it online, we're following the prompts created by others. One click leads to another, by design, and all of it is directed by someone else: the software engineer or the media giant or the advertiser or the Instagram poster who's giving you FOMO or the manipulative bot army of another government. It has all been designed to lure us in, based on everything it knows about us. And it knows a lot.

Letting our minds wander online—immersed in the thoughts and wishes of someone else—is far less likely to end in a big, new insight than in buying something we might not even need. Yes, there are times when I am led to links that teach me new or unusual things . . . but that's not always the case.

Other forms of guided mind wandering can be useful. Reading a novel, watching a movie: these also transport us to places others have designed. They provide an opportunity to view the world through another's eyes, and, as research has made clear, they can increase our sense of empathy.[15] Storytelling is a powerful tool for increasing human connection. But the guided mind wandering we do online is different. It's guided not by storytelling but by commerce, political agendas, and other suspect motives. Books and movies don't (yet) have in-app purchases, but the sites you visit in your online wanderings sure do. With smartphones in our hands at all times, how many hours of mind wandering are we losing? What are we missing out on by forgetting to just stare out the window? That should be the real FOMO. Wouldn't we all like a scientific excuse to just do nothing? So now, when I'm standing in line, I try to think, *Don't reach for the device.* It doesn't always work, but . . . I try. My internal narrator reminds me of what I might lose.

―――――――

One of my favorite ways to take my mind out to play is to go to a conference to hear a talk. I spend a lot of my career both listening to talks and giving them. There are some speakers who have me completely riveted and focused. But even then, they are sparking tangents in my own mind.

I was recently at a talk in a vintage theater with ornate carvings flanking the stage in downtown LA. Normally, when I'm at a talk, I sit in the front row so there are no distractions between me and the stage. But this time I was late, so I snuck into the last row. And here's what I saw ahead of me: all the glowing screens of people on social media or texting.

No wonder I was so unsettled in the back row of that talk. There were hundreds of screens drawing my attention away, and instead of focusing on the lecture or enjoying my own daydream, I was thinking about what all the other attendees were losing out on, eyes glued to their smartphones.

―――――――

The default mode network can take us to magical places. But we also have to get things accomplished, and when we do, the brain's other primary process takes over. This is called the task positive network, and it switches on whenever you're focused on a project. While the default mode network gets activated when we let our minds wander, the task positive network gets activated when we pay attention. When you're deep in conversation, absorbed in an activity, or trying to solve a problem, the task positive network is in charge. It's essentially the opposite of the default mode network. The two networks are mutually exclusive: when one is active, the other is dormant.

If you meditate, you've felt your brain switch over. When you start, you're still in default mode network, and your thoughts are all over the place. But as you push those stray thoughts aside and begin to focus, the task positive network kicks in.

While the default mode network can take us to the past and future, the task positive network is all about the present. It's what takes in the here and now. On my screen-free day, I toggle between the two. I spend a lot of time daydreaming in the default mode network, but also want to be present in the moment, which is where the task positive network comes in. The task positive network also processes sensory input, so I try to make sure the moment is pretty great by devoting the day to tasks and sensory experiences I really enjoy.

Though they're essentially polar opposites, both of these modes play important roles in brain function. And they're *both* disrupted by screens. Picking up a phone when we're in the task positive network distracts us right out of it. Phones also pull us out when we're in the default mode network and spacing out in a good way. None of this is good for cognition, creativity, productivity, or general well-being.

So this is my case to spend more time in your "networks" that allow you to be creative and present. The more you understand how they work, the more you will treat them with care and respect. Just like a switch on your phone to put it into airplane mode, the way you can activate and strengthen these modes is by giving them more time to flourish.

15

Silence and Stillness

"Silence isn't empty, it's full of answers."

—UNKNOWN

As a working parent who feels like my days are spent swinging from branches through the noisy forests of home, schools, and work, I am starved for silence. So it's wonderful to find environments where I can concentrate. Heschel describes the Sabbath as a palace in time. I found my perfect palace in space: the library. With its soaring ceilings of painted sherbet clouds and blue skies ten stories high encouraging expansive thoughts, the New York Public Library is an ideal place to write. Majestic lion statues flank the grand entrance as if they're guarding something quiet and revered against the hustle and bustle of Manhattan. The book-lined walls surround you with ideas from history's great thinkers, doors to a thousand different worlds. The silence of that vast space lets you think and feel, imagine and hear. I also find that kind of quiet sanctuary in my hometown library, nestled in redwoods, or when I get up early to write—before the kids (or even the birds) have woken up.

Most of the time, however, the world is full of noise. Think of our soundscape as a spectrum, with a wall of sound like a rock concert on the left, and silence all the way to the right. In between you have the bustle of a big, noisy party, the droning talking heads of news shows, the chirps of our digital devices, a lecture in a hushed auditorium, an intimate conversation late at night with your partner; and then at the very end, you alone in silence, perhaps unable to sleep.

It's no surprise that human beings need silence. This is true even on a biological level. Sound activates the amygdala, resulting in the release of the stress hormone cortisol. Studies have linked chronic noise to increased rates of heart disease and high blood pressure. A 2011 study conducted by the World Health Organization attributed three thousand heart disease deaths annually to the effects of noise pollution. (It makes sense that the word "noise" derives from the same Latin word as "nausea," meaning "sickness.") Silence, conversely, promotes cell development in the hippocampus, the part of the brain that controls memory and sensory processing. During silent times, the brain can process its backlog of information. A study led by Duke University biologist Imke Kirste showed that two hours a day of silent time was enough to produce these cognitive benefits.[16]

But silence can be hard to come by. No wonder people are seeking silence in retreats like Sweden's 72-Hour Cabins, off-grid glass houses that look like clear jewelry boxes sitting in the forest, and Getaway's bandwidth-free cabins near Shenandoah National Park and other locations. The Appalachian town of Green Bank, known as the quietest town in America, has banned cell phones and Wi-Fi entirely.

Most of us have to make our silent sanctuaries ourselves. We seek these pockets of stillness and spaces for focused attention so we can think in absolute quiet, or so we can listen. I think that's part of what's behind the recent popularity of podcasts, which lend themselves to what *On Being* host Krista Tippett calls "deep and generous listening." It's always interesting to see humanity's attempt at homeostasis. In the mid-'90s, when computers had us slumping toward screens, the yoga revolution arrived to stretch us back. It was a healing response to physical atrophy. Now that we're constantly subjected to electric notification buzz-shock treatment, we're turning to podcasts, just you and the voice directly into your ear, with nothing between you and the podcaster's words and thoughts.

Out in the world, however, we sometimes are unwilling eavesdroppers, forced to overhear others' conversations. At other times we may be the loud ones. Many of us also struggle with our own internal negative narrator. Needless to say, we have a lot of simultaneous narratives to manage. Let's return to Heschel's palace in time. On our weekly day off the network we really get to create our figurative palace. For me, it starts with a lively dinner of connection and then, the next day, with room for silence and introspection. It's such a nice break from the buzzes, rings, and dings that rule the week. During silent times, the brain can go into the default mode network. Silence improves cognition, and it gives the brain a much-needed break.

It gives our bodies a break, too. Studies suggest that silence, meditation, and rest promote longevity. We know that people who keep a rest day tend to live longer. (As a number of studies have shown, Seventh Day Adventists, who keep a weekly Sabbath, live ten years longer than the average American.) One reason may be the effect unplugging has on our telomeres, the tips of our chromosomes that shorten as we get older and produce the symptoms of aging. But restful practices like meditation can help reverse this. Studies done by Elissa Epel and Nobel Prize–winning biologist Elizabeth Blackburn have shown that meditation can help lengthen telomeres, while exposure to stress shortens them.[17]

Stillness and quiet are integral to so many spiritual beliefs and religions, from monastic vows of silence to the Muslim practice of *muraqabah*, or quiet mindfulness. Silence and reflection are a central part of Buddhist philosophy, too. One of my favorite Buddhist images pictures the soul as a body of water with wind blowing across it. It sparkles and reflects and refracts light all around it. In this state, you can't see what's inside the water, just everything around it. It is only when you still the wind on the water that you can see what's inside.

For me, that stillness is what these days of rest are all about. They let us see what's inside the water.

16

Gratitude and Practice

I am a big journal writer and have been since I was a kid, from the bubble-cursive elementary entries to the angst-filled entries of my teens and early twenties: "My heart is broken." "I ran out of money on my film . . . again." Reading the entries from that period, I wonder how I ever got out of bed in the morning. From that time on, I decided to write across all kinds of emotional states: happy, inspired, sad, or any of the range of moods that color my days. It's like I'm a reporter for my own life trying to figure it out.

Journaling is how I practice presence, cultivate gratitude, create my sense of self, work to stay grounded, and determine what I want to do and what I want to work on. It's also my way to sort out what's happened in my life and the world at large. I can process the joys and chaos of my week, and the ups and downs of life.

As research is showing, journaling really can improve your life in concrete ways. (Although that was not why I started doing it, it certainly explains why it felt so grounding to do.) The benefits of journaling are supported by several studies that show it promotes better sleep, a stronger immune system, and even a higher IQ. It can actually help you recover from injury faster.

As for gratitude, focusing on being thankful has been shown to help people reduce stress, sleep better, and improve their health. Among adolescents, it's been shown to increase generosity and decrease materialism.[18]

Gratitude activates the hypothalamus, which controls emotional regulation and cues the release of dopamine, the "reward" hormone. When we *express* gratitude, as opposed to just practicing it, the benefits increase (this is why I'm a great believer in handwritten thank-you notes). In one 2017 study, a group that practiced and expressed gratitude reported better outcomes than the group that only practiced it.[19] Expressing gratitude seems to be especially important in maintaining healthy relationships: several studies have shown that hearing a partner express gratitude made people feel more loved, comfortable, and grateful themselves. So on Tech Shabbat, we express it. We write about it. Unlike the Orthodox Jewish practice of Shabbat (no electricity, work, writing, or creation of any kind), our version includes journaling and other creative activities. For us, this is the essence of Shabbat: being thankful and present.

Every Saturday morning, Ken and I start the day by writing about the best parts of our week. We make coffee—"black gold," as Ken calls it—and pull out a collection of journals and pads of paper and pens. We fill pages with things we appreciated from that week, like *holding hands with Blooma roller-skating under a disco ball, solving a math problem with Odessa, going to the farmers market and seeing persimmons are in season,* and *Ken and I laughing about the new organization we want to start: "The Association of Free Association."* The more specific we can be about the things that made us laugh, pause, or smile, the better. These wonderful little moments are so easy to forget, but when we remember them and write them down, they let us stretch out the moment and linger on the best parts of life.

Some people do extreme sports; I do extreme journaling. I have a cornucopia of different journals for different kinds of writing. One lets me take a big-picture look back on each week, one lets me record little moments of gratitude, and one just documents the things that made me laugh. Ken jokes that I need a journal just to keep track of my journals.

On Saturday morning Ken and I do our gratitude journaling, me in a journal labeled "Unplug" and Ken in one titled "Appreciation," because he thinks the word "gratitude" is corny.

On our screen-free day, we have a lot to "appreciate." If we spend too much of our time during the week scrolling through news feeds, focused on the worst of what happens in our world, Tech Shabbat lets us focus on the best. It gives us perspective: on gratitude, being present, and valuing what we have right in front of us.

Just like anything, cultivating gratitude takes time and attention. On our one day off of screens, we have a lot of both, and everything we experience seems to present itself as something to be grateful for, appreciate, or not take for granted.

This practice spills over into the week. I've set up my day with prompts to think thankful thoughts. A quote from Benjamin Disraeli leaning on the mirror above my sink proclaims: "Never take anything for granted." When I brush my teeth, it reminds me to be grateful for my hands holding the toothbrush, my teeth, the ability to afford a toothbrush, a roof over my head, and everything else I'm lucky to have. Sometimes my eyes don't process it because I see it there every day, but I would say around half the time, I read and absorb those words. This visual prompt helps. In the kitchen, a quote on the refrigerator by Cesare Pavese says: "We do not remember days, we remember moments," reminding me to be grateful for small things. It's one thing not to sweat the small stuff, but another to actually savor them. At the end of the day, when I close my eyes to go to sleep, I focus on three things I am grateful for. It helps me to not stress and to sleep better. Heschel said, "Our goal should be to live life in radical amazement . . . get up in the morning and look at the world in a way that takes nothing for granted."

I found gratitude journaling so helpful for my overall mood and framing for each day that I decided to do it the other six days, too. Of course, those are the six days when I have less time. So let me introduce you to a new form of gratitude journaling that I have found to be profound in its simplicity and the short amount of time it takes: . . . [*pen drumroll*] . . . Alex Ikonn and UJ Ramda's *The Five-Minute Journal*, which describes itself as "the journal for people who don't write in journals." The author even says, "This is a journal for people who don't write in journals." Basically, you write for a couple of minutes to start your day and a couple of minutes to end your day—five minutes total—and your day is like a gratitude sandwich, with these pages the slices of appreciation. I love it.

My mother is my role model for this practice. My favorite memories of my mom are of her snuggled in bed surrounded by anything a curious person could want: a pile of books, reading glasses, pens to underline and highlight, a collection of different notepads with vintage postcards stuck on their covers—some for words she likes, one for quotes, another for ideas—and a glass jar of lemon drops. These are the tools she uses to preserve bits of wisdom or observations that will endure, like fossils, long after everything else is gone. As I now have my own collection of these items, I realize she has modeled a way of enjoying life, savoring ideas, writing down feelings, and finding the hidden gems of knowledge that have been passed down to me, my siblings, and her grandchildren.

Writing down thoughts, stories, and things that have happened is especially important among families. As Bruce Feiler writes in *The Secrets of Happy Families*, families who share stories—who have a narrative—do better, even when there are hardships. Hearing about your grandparents' struggles as new immigrants, your parents' college shenanigans, your rogue great-uncle's arrest for stealing a horse—all these stories bind you together, tell you who you are, and give you a script to follow when the next hardship comes.

When it does, these practices—storytelling, journaling, and gratitude—give you the tools to deal with them. They provide a way to quiet all the negativity and the noise that surrounds us—especially when we're on screens. These little gems of gratitude are also like tranquilizers for the negative narrator in our heads. Then there's the deeper inner voice that you can hear more clearly when you quiet your ongoing narrator and write things down—the voice that tries to remind you to live your truth, telling you to do all the things you need to do before you die. "That person is *the one*." "Quit that job." "Make that film." "Write that book." "Volunteer more." "Run for office." "Get off the screens." Whatever it may be.

We have so much to be grateful for. We often think the world is going downhill, but the truth, on the whole, is that it's not. Steven

Pinker, in his book *The Better Angels of Our Nature*, has shown that the rate of violence around the world has actually declined throughout history. Prehistoric people had about a 50 percent chance of being killed by another human, and that's obviously not the case now. Pinker's theory about why we perceive the world as being so violent is, first, that the news only reports what *does* happen, not what doesn't happen, and second, that we just care more about each death, because we're more connected than ever before.

Which brings us back to Ken's word, "appreciation." Pinker proposes that appreciation is key to building a better world: "I would say that it's appreciating the progress that gives us the courage and conviction to try to strive for more progress. History tells us that attempts to make the world better tend to succeed. We'll never achieve a utopia, but that doesn't mean we can't make things a little bit better."

Of course, I wrote this down in one of my journals.

It can be hard to see the plot of your life when you're in it. Taking a break once a week closes a chapter. It gives you a chance to see where the story of your life, of your family, has gone so far, and to think about where you want it to go next. When I do my Saturday journaling, I get all that down on the page.

The word "culture" comes from the Latin word *colere*, which means "to cultivate the soil." Giving yourself time to cultivate this practice of reflecting on your week, writing down what you appreciate, what you are grateful for, and saying it out loud, is the fertilizer. To paraphrase a quote, "Gratitude is like manure: the more you spread it around, the more things grow"—for yourself, your relationships, and ultimately your engagement in the world and contribution to culture in a more rooted place. And gratitude smells much better.

17

Nature and Perspective

In the 1970s, a group of Jews transplanted from Detroit that included my parents decided to take the High Holiday services outside. Instead of inside a stuffy synagogue, they'd hold their services on top of Mount Tamalpais in an outdoor stone amphitheater, which had hosted one of the first outdoor rock festivals. They called it "Temple Without Walls."

To four-year-old me, it was epic and beautiful. Along with more than a hundred people on the top of that mountain, I was sweating under my fancy felt dress, but I was happy. I'm not a religious person, but there, amid the live oak and madrone trees, overlooking the Pacific Ocean, the vastness of the sky, I felt connected to something larger than myself. I still do.

The closest articulation of how I feel about nature and spirituality is from Albert Einstein: "I prefer an attitude of humility corresponding to the weakness of our intellectual understanding of nature and of our own being." That pretty much sums it up for me. Thank you, Albert Einstein, for conveying the General Theory of Agnosticity.

When my family started keeping Tech Shabbats, it made perfect sense that we'd incorporate nature into the practice. Nothing connects me spiritually like being outdoors: going on a river-rafting trip down the Grand Canyon, hiking through Muir Woods, going swimming, experiencing the awe of a multi-hued sunset, or even sitting in my garden. We try to make being in nature a regular part of our screen-free day. It's one of the benefits I'm most grateful for. It really does get me, and my family, out more.

Collectively, however, we're spending a lot less time outside, and it appears screens are the reason why. One recent study revealed that children ages eight to twelve spend three times as much time on screens as they do playing outside. Adults, meanwhile, are in nature fewer than five hours a week.[20]

This is unfortunate, because being outdoors has so many advantages. If you've ever returned from a stroll through a city park or from a hike feeling rebalanced, you know this firsthand. As it turns out, there's a scientific reason that spending time in nature makes us feel calm, centered, and connected. It's known as "soft fascination," and it happens in places like parks, where the brain is engaged but not overtaxed. Studies suggest that people who live near green spaces have lower levels of the stress hormone cortisol. EEGs performed on volunteers while they walked showed brain activity that was markedly more serene when they were in nature than when they walked through urban spaces.[21] And a number of studies show that children do better on tests when they spend time walking in nature first.

Being in nature also creates a feeling of awe that in turn makes us more empathetic and generous. In one study, after participants were sent to a grove of enormous eucalyptus trees, they exhibited more prosocial behavior. The researchers theorized that the awe induced by the towering trees reminded the subjects of their role in the larger world.[22]

The benefits of being in nature are well known and celebrated in Japan, where the practice of *shirin-yoku*—"forest bathing," meaning spending time in nature—is common and widely encouraged. A 2018 book on the subject by Dr. Qing Li documents its many benefits: forest bathing can improve heart health, immune response, and overall well-being, while reducing anxiety, stress, and depression.

Being outside makes me feel more attuned and linked to the natural world. Which in turn links me to the world as a whole. It's sort of ironic—by disconnecting from screens, I feel more connected to everything and everyone.

This is true on an environmental level. As my friend Yosef Abramovitz says, "Shabbat is radically eco-conscious. If everyone truly didn't consume for one day a week, we could get close to solving climate change." Instead of using, buying, disposing, on our Tech Shabbats we take time to preserve, appreciate, focus.

———

There is an unfortunate saying, "dumb as dirt," but even dirt knows you have to take time off; if you plant the same plot over and over, you'll use up all its nutrients. (Dirt is pretty miraculous, actually. Add water and a seed and incredible things happen— just like our brains.)

Judaism has a concept called *shmittah*, which is sort of like a Shabbat for the soil. Every seventh year, you're commanded to give the land the whole year off so it has a chance to recover from supporting six years of crops. So every seven years, give the land a break. *Shmittah* is also similar to the concept of the sabbatical. Academics have this great idea that every seven years you need to take a break from your everyday work to rest, reset, and refresh your mind. "Sabbatical" actually takes its name from "Sabbath."

When Ken had his first sabbatical in 2005, we spent a month in Hana, Hawaii, trading houses with his cousin. Hana is a tropical paradise on the island of Maui. It is far away from the tourists, thanks to a twisty, windy road that will make you carsick but also awestruck, as waterfalls and rainbows are revealed just when you think you won't make it.

It was a magical time, made more magical by the fact that we were spending our time off in such a wonderful natural environment. We ate ripe papayas, passion fruit, and avocados that fell from the trees, and any fish the fishermen caught and sold from their trucks off the beach that day.

Since Hana is on the rainforest side of the island, there are deep, thunderous, dramatic rainstorms each day. It was the best kind of white noise. I slept so well there. (I heard that sometimes people come to Hana just to sleep.) Days were filled with going to the beach, reading, painting watercolors, and teaching Odessa about the names of the stars: the Big and Little Dippers and Orion's Belt. What a gift that we got to be away from our busy lives for one month to either do nothing or think deeply. Different soil, different smells, different insights.

The night we drove out of this sabbatical wonderland, on that same windy road with our temporary life stuffed in our rental car, we heard little Odessa, strapped in her car seat, laughing uncontrollably. Nothing like listening to your two-year-old amusing herself. When she finally was able to breathe and tell us what was so funny, she said, "Orion just pooped a star." She'd seen her first shooting star. We laughed our way through those twisty roads back to civilization. Then we returned to California, recharged and ready.

We've managed to do a sabbatical only two other times since then, but now we have these weekly mini-sabbaticals in the form of our screen-free day, and it's both doable and enough.

Today, we as a society need to catch our breath and focus again. Which brings us back to *colere*, to cultivate and care for. When we care for ourselves through rest and nature, we advance culture, too.

18

Memory and Time

Growing up in the '70s, my childhood was recorded by Polaroids, the newest, most exciting camera technology of the time. So much happened off camera, but those overexposed squares with rainbow chemical leaks on the image are what I remember most.

Now we can take tens of thousands of pictures and videos, and we store them away on machines and in the cloud. Capturing memories and storing them became cheap and accessible. We're recording so much more. How much are we actually remembering?

Earlier I described rest as a form of technology. Memory is a technology, too. It's our own personal hard drive, and its contents define who we are. Without our memories, we have no sense of personal identity, relationships, and our role in the world.

The way we use memory has evolved as our culture has. When literacy arrived and let us outsource a lot of our mental RAM to written records, people worried. Plato was afraid that the invention of writing would make people lose their memory. I imagine him lamenting in a toga, "Everyone used to know *The Iliad* by heart. But no one memorizes anything anymore. Everyone's on their tablets, reading and writing all the time, forgetting the great texts." (A far cry from our current-day definition of "tablets" and "texts.")

Within a short time, Plato's fears were realized, but culture marched ahead all the same, with information being passed down in books to create a whole new body of knowledge. People panicked again when computers arrived. Computers—which have their own "memory"—let us outsource even more. With the arrival of smartphones, we have to remember even less, including our most important phone numbers. I can recite the phone number of my childhood home as well as five of my best friends' childhood homes from nearly forty years ago, but I can't recite the five phone numbers I call most today.

Which reminds me of something my father used to tell me about Einstein, that shows outsourcing some memory isn't necessarily a bad thing. When a colleague asked him for his phone number, the story goes, Einstein got out a phone book, opened it to the Es, ran his finger down the list of names, then said, "There it is: Albert Einstein." The colleague was aghast, wondering how the smartest man in the world could not know his own telephone number. But to Einstein it made perfect sense. By not filling his brain with facts that he could find elsewhere, he'd have more space to think about bigger ideas. Like, say, the theory of relativity.

That was seventy years before the Internet. How much more mental room are we freeing up today with access to so much storage online? As we're outsourcing so much of our memory, what are we gaining and what are we losing? If memory is an evolving technology, what does that mean today? And how does living 24/6 affect how memory works?

Taking a day off from all screens every week actually does

affect memory in many positive ways. Neuroscientists tell us that by resting and relaxing and slowing down the input of new information, we're giving our brains a chance to recover and sort. The result is improved memory and better recall. It's sort of like we're cleaning out our mental file cabinets every week.

The weekly break is also an opportunity to let our memories evolve. Memories change over time. This is true on both a cultural level (the movie we remember loving twenty years ago now seems sexist) and a personal one. Our brains and our world are constantly evolving, which means our memories are, too. Being stored in neurons is very different from being carved in stone. Every time you activate those neurons by recalling a given memory, you change it, sometimes subtly, sometimes dramatically, as you learn and experience more and get more context, infusing new information into the old. What was once a bad memory can become a good one, and vice versa. As neuroscientist Rosalind Cartwright writes, "Memory is never a precise duplicate of the original; instead, it is a continuing act of creation."

We are constantly editing our memories. Our memories strengthen and change depending on how much time we devote to thinking—and *rethinking*—each moment. I'm always going back to old journals to revisit my thoughts. (One of the things I like to do is to identify what I was worried about that didn't come into fruition, to try to teach me to worry less.)

When I was living 24/7, life was flying by. Quantity ruled. More hours meant more productivity. More value. More worth. When my family and I started taking that day off, I saw that it allowed the best memories to linger. And it's no coincidence that most of those best memories fall on my screen-free day. Partly, that's because it's happening when I'm doing my favorite things with my favorite people, but it's also because I'm receptive to it. I'm actually going to remember what happens that day because the impression won't be replaced by the tweet I saw, the stressful headline that I can't stop thinking about, or an email that requires my focus. I won't miss experiencing the event because I'm too busy recording it, and my memories won't be displaced by pictures of the day. A recent study confirmed that we remember things less well when we use screens to document them.[23] The researchers describe the process: "Creating a hard copy of an experience through media leaves only a diminished copy in our own heads."

How is that affecting us? Are we actually changing the way our memory works? And if we are, how do we make that a gain rather than a loss?

———

As the resident filmmaker in my family, I'm the one who makes short movies documenting all the big milestones: my father's and mother's seventieth birthdays, Ken's fiftieth, our best friends' fortieths. (It's interesting that no matter how old someone is, or how big a milestone we are celebrating, their life seems to make a seven-minute film, not much over, not much under.) This means capturing key moments on video, then combining them with old photos to make a short movie about someone's life. These are truly labors of love. It takes months to hunt down the ruffled-edged photos, Polaroids, and shots from Instamatics stored in attics and garages around the country. I am the film editor, arranging their lives and memories into a narrative we'll watch and celebrate.

The most meaningful film was the last one I made for my dad.

Right before he died, he told me he had an idea and asked me, like any good accomplice, would I help him carry it out?

I filmed him in a white suit, the one he wore to his wedding to my stepmother, Ina, and I created a makeshift green-screen studio in my living room that I'd later replace with clouds. He looked like George Burns in the 1977 film *Oh, God!* Even though he was so sick during that period, it was as if he parted the heavy chemo fog for the three hours the camera was on, as animated and present as ever. He said all the things he wanted to say to me, my brother, my sister, our kids, Ina, her kids, his friends, and his family.

On his deathbed, when he couldn't speak, he squeezed my hand in a conspiratorial way, as we both had this secret that he knew it was almost time to reveal.

A few days later, we all were at the temple for his funeral, wearing torn black fabric squares pinned to our clothing like a flock of crows. (This Jewish custom represents how the fabric of your life will forever be torn by their death.) A gospel performer sang "Ain't No Mountain High Enough" while everyone clapped along, off beat. Close family and friends were all seated on the raised platform at different stages of crying or expressing our love for him. I made my way to the podium with both hands cradling my nine-months-pregnant belly, crying so hard I barely got the words out: "My father always said he wanted to be at his own funeral, so here he is."

FADE UP on the large projection screen that appeared to my right. My father, in his white suit in front of perfect clouds, full of life, smiles and says, "Hi, everyone. I always wanted to attend my own funeral, so here I am."

The shocked and delighted mourners burst into laughter through the tears. Then he said all that he wanted and told us goodbye. He paused, and you could hear his voice crack to reveal a vast chasm of pain and affection as he said, "I love you all, and I'm really going to miss you. But this is the way it is. I'll always be with you."

FADE OUT. Then the film montage of his life played.

He got to write his own ending. He got to choose the memory he left us with.

————

Though we don't realize it, we're all writing our lives every day, in the big choices and the thousands of little choices we make, the things we say and do, all of it adding up to a memory that exists only in neurons—our own and others'.

Our memories are what connect us to ourselves, others, and our place in the world. Let's do more things that leave deep imprints. I used to think only those Polaroid photo moments had carved deep memories, but the things I remember most from when I was young weren't recorded on film: the Sunday breakfasts, walking to school through the woods with my siblings, or discussions after going to the movies. Now the deepest memories mostly come from our screen-free days. We won't have any pictures of them, but we won't forget them, either.

What do you want to remember? And how do you want people to remember you?

PART VI:
THE BIG PICTURE

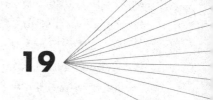

19

A More Balanced Web

As a mother, a feminist, and someone who's been in the tech world since the early days of the Web, I'm not surprised that we are at a moment of reckoning for both tech and gender. Though there are, and always have been, pioneering women in technology, there aren't as many as there should be. And there certainly weren't enough women in the room when the Web's business models were built back in the late '90s. Our devices, systems, and products were designed by a pretty monochromatic group that does not represent the population their inventions serve and affect.

While there was so much focus on "monetizing eyeballs" and making websites "sticky," little thought was given to the consequences of eyeballs that stuck too much. How would having screens everywhere change the world? How would it affect our children? How would it affect us? This lack of intentionality about the impact of this technology has created significant problems: in how we spend our time (win at all costs by keeping people addicted to screens at all costs), in workplace culture (the expectation to be on 24/7), and in the seeming lack of concern for the fallout (burnout, privacy violations, and election hacking).

Across the board, there's a lack of balance: the speed at which the technology is taking over is so much greater than the speed at which we're able to grasp its impact. And the people in the room making the decisions are rarely connected to the people in homes, feeling the effects. How do we fix that?

For these systems to flourish in the years ahead, it's vital that we think back to the original vision of the Web and do a better job of integrating significantly more diverse perspectives into the creation of these products and devices, and that we think through—and legislate—the outcomes more carefully. Just as our political leaders ought to reflect the people they are representing, the people at the forefront of the Web and the designers of our devices and apps should reflect the people who use them—because this makes things better for *everyone*. As Matt Ridley observes in his 2010 book, *The Rational Optimist*, innovation happens more often where diverse populations with different perspectives and experiences collide—in cities, at universities, at cafes, at intersections of humanity. If necessity is the mother of invention, its fairy godmother is diversity.

Ada Lovelace, the first proto-computer programmer, knew this well. She said that imagination "seizes points in common, between subjects having no very apparent connexion, & hence seldom or never brought into juxtaposition."

A diversity of perspectives means not only diversity in terms of gender, race, class, and geography but also in the spectrum of skills that different people bring. This includes those like engineering and programming, as well as "soft skills"—cooperation, collaboration, intuition, empathy, storytelling, connection, creativity, gratitude, and the desire to nurture—all just as important as software. And although all these skills are crucial to culture, commerce, and everyday life, traditionally, they've been undervalued.

Even the term "soft skills" sells them short, contrasting them with "hard skills," whose name suggests they are more difficult to master and that they are also more important and indispensable. But to be good at empathy and social intelligence takes work and rigor. It's not "soft" at all. Valuing these skills starts in our education systems. STEM-focused education (science, technology, engineering, and math), while it has tremendous benefits, has been promoted as the only path to success, as if the lingua franca of the future will be only numbers, formulas, and lines of code. But these tools grow in their power and usefulness when they are combined with the skills provided by artists, designers, writers, teachers, communicators, and cultural creators. They are the ones who can make new technologies accessible, sustainable, and beneficial to society at large.

Some educators have already added an *A* for "arts" (STEAM). Odessa suggests that we add an *H* for "humanities," and I'd add a *C* for "conscience." Not STEM, not STEAM, but SCHTEAM (which I like because it sounds Yiddish).

The process of considering soft skills, consequences, and diversity needs to be a focus at every stage of tech development, from funding, to leadership, to rollout, to oversight. To keep us from being just raw material for employers, marketers, and people or governments with corrupt political goals to exploit. It's gone too far, and it's time to reverse course. As Jaron Lanier said in his 2018 TED talk, "How We Need to Remake the Internet": "We cannot have a society in which, if two people wish to communicate, the only way that can happen is if it's financed by a third person who wishes to manipulate them." Let's take a careful look at which parts of new technologies are making our lives better and which parts are making them worse.

For example: Today, we almost never find ourselves in ad-free environments. Everywhere we look, there are billboards and logos and pop-ups encouraging us to buy this or that. In Brazil, citizens of São Paolo decided they'd had enough and in 2006 voted to ban all outdoor ads. The city is now routinely described as "quiet" and "clean." Imagine if we put restrictions on online ads as well.

Advertising has its own agenda, and it's very effective. Now that we see the results—the loss of privacy and the manipulation to keep us on screens as much as possible—it's become clear that free services haven't been free at all. In fact, the costs can be enormous, especially when these privacy violations and models of manipulation are used to undermine our democracy. While the huge issue of how our data is being sold and used is something we need to address, there are some models for change. Some sites that have managed to avoid the ad trap and data sellout are both crowd-funded and crowdsourced. Crowdsourcing by definition brings together multiple perspectives.

The best example of a site that's doing that well is Wikipedia. Wikipedia really did fulfill the promise of the Web. It's a digital version of the libraries of Alexandria—a gathering place to find, share, and debate all the world's information. It is participatory and accessible to all. (Sometimes you can see that struggle in real time if you look at the edit history of a Wikipedia entry.) When the window pops up on my browser at the end of the year to donate for this great service, our family is glad to contribute. Let's create more examples of meaningful services that we wouldn't hesitate to pay for. Think about the free online services you use every day that you pay for with your privacy. What monthly fee would you pay for that same service to protect your privacy and build a healthier Web?

This shift to thinking through the unintended consequences of technology needs participation from all aspects of our society—corporate, legislative, and personal. Technology companies need to think about their ethical philosophy, and hire executives who make this their sole focus. In addition to a chief executive officer (CEO), for example, what if corporations appointed a chief *ethics* officer and a chief *empathy* officer, who can act as thoughtful, conscious brakes, so that the leadership has the time to consider the impact of developing technologies and their effects on diverse populations, one, five, ten years out. What good things might come of this new technology? What bad things? How might we circumvent undesirable outcomes? These positions aren't the antidote to technologies created, but they are an important step that can help companies focus on not just the product but its result. And when, inevitably, companies create problems for people and society, we need better systems for developing diverse oversight boards that include a combination of affected citizens, watchdog groups, community leaders, and elected officials. The more diverse voices, the better.

When it comes to rules and regulations, the first step is acknowledgment and awareness. Tech advances are happening so fast that legislation simply hasn't kept up. Nor are the people legislating necessarily equipped to make those decisions. In many ways technology is uncharted territory with a foreign language native to a tiny minority of people. In order to get ahead of this problem, we'd benefit from more transparency, and more people

dedicated to translating between technologies and their consequences. Let's hold more public forums in addition to the con-
gressional hearings. Let's get up to speed, before the problem runs
too far away from us.

It's time for more balance across the board—for industry, for
government, and for ourselves. Because this is a personal reckoning for each of us, too, to own our role in all of this, something
we have intimate control over. How can we do things in the way
we live that will restore balance? How can we make our own rules
and regulations to help us get there?

20

Thinking Backwards

> "History is an angel being blown backwards into the
> future."
>
> —WALTER BENJAMIN
> VIA LAURIE ANDERSON

"Let's think backwards" is a phrase I use when I want to think through all the steps toward a goal, whether it's making a film, planning one of our global conversations, or just trying to get through the day's commitments on time and in the right frame of mind. The idea is to start with the ultimate goal, and then figure out the steps to get there.

Here, let's think about the long-term future, the world we want to live in, and then identify the steps we need to take as individuals and as a society to make that happen. The issues surrounding technology are intergenerational, global, complex, and incredibly difficult to frame and diagnose, much less solve. But it is important to try, and I believe 24/6 living could be one (of many) steps along that path.

What unplugging lets us do, essentially, is reflect on the past, present, and future. It gives us the space to ask: *What are the strengths we value in our society? What are the strengths we value in ourselves? And how can we reinforce both?*

Thousands of years ago, when people worried about the future, they put questions to oracles. Today, let's put the questions less to search engines and more to ourselves, if we want to ensure a good future for our generation and the coming ones. The next ten to one hundred years may produce technological innovations we never could have imagined. It will require a lot more people to think about and create these solutions as well: by 2100, it's predicted there will be 11.2 billion people on the planet, all of them connected by an even more powerful Internet. Just thinking about how radically our way of life has changed in the past one hundred years gives you an idea of how different this future world could be. (It's stunning how different life is now. Around a hundred years ago, you could die from a paper cut. Women couldn't vote. People commuted by horse.) Using that as perspective, let's imagine two futures: the one that is coming our way if we continue down this path of being accessible to and influenced by everyone and everything 24/7 and one that is the future we actually *want*.

———

Some future realities are obvious: the world will be increasingly automated, digital, and connected. But that doesn't mean humans will be obsolete; just the opposite, in fact. It will be our most human qualities that are most valuable, as these can't and shouldn't be outsourced to machines. For example, computers and AI have a hard time with context. Humans generally understand what a person is saying even if their words and physical expressions contradict each other. They also know when it's okay to bend the rules, when it's time to try something new. Bots can't make these sorts of intuitive calls, but you can. All your experiences and education are what give you that very unique and very human ability.

I was recently at the Metropolitan Museum of Art in New York City, which has two million square feet of sacred objects from hundreds of different civilizations. You can tell a lot about a society by what it worships. Today, it seems that we are worshipping devices, robots, and artificial intelligence, with hopes and fears for what they will do for us in the future. We're simultaneously in awe of our inventions and also fearful that they will someday render us irrelevant. And many sensational news headlines fuel that narrative.

It makes me wonder what the Met will be full of a thousand years from now. How will people from the future interpret what we're idolizing and projecting our hopes and fears on today?

Ken has spent the last two decades as a professor of AI and robotics, countering the argument that machines and artificial intelligence will replace people. Instead, he predicts that computers will complement human skills and relieve us of some of the tedious aspects of our jobs. So yes, while repetitive jobs will most likely disappear, they will be replaced by more multifaceted ones.[24] Meaning the skills we'll value in the future—the skills we should be focusing on now in our education systems and through our interaction with technology—are the skills that machines don't have: curiosity, creativity, empathy, critical thinking, adaptability.

These are *exactly* the skills we develop by living a 24/6 life.

On Saturdays, when we detach from the screens, machines, and the enormous primal-urge network, we not only strengthen the skills that will become increasingly valuable in an automated age, we're also better able to see, and feel, the personal and emotional changes that come from being online and on screens so much. Which brings us back to these questions: What are the strengths we value in society? And what are the strengths we value in ourselves? Is this short-attention-spanned, reactive, screen-addicted place somewhere good for us? Is it where we want to be?

One of my favorite things my father used to say was, "If you're not living on the edge, you're taking up way too much space." And I think right now, "living on the edge" means spending more time unplugged, with more time to think and time to be. The devices have taken over, and we've come to a place where we are responding to them, rather than the other way around. We need to detach, go to that edge, and look in from the outside to see how it's transforming us.

The Web arrived only recently. And it has a lot of evolving left to do. All the parts aren't even connected yet. If we think of the Web as a brain—which I like to do—the part we are currently using most is like the oldest, most primal, reptilian core of the brain (the amygdala), the run-from-beast part that kept humans alive until the more cautious and thoughtful prefrontal cortex—the part of the brain that governs impulse control—came along. The prefrontal cortex acts as a brake. The Internet doesn't really have that . . . yet.

To further the brain analogy, neuroscience shows us that a child doesn't have their first big insight until all the different parts of the brain are connected. During that period, the brain is adding and pruning connections at breakneck speed, and it is in need of constant nurturing attention to grow properly. I believe we're just coming out of that stage with the Web, and are now moving into the teenage years: easily distracted, excited and excitable, always looking for something new, and a little too interested in sex. In those teenage years, the prefrontal cortex is still outweighed by the amygdala, but it's fighting hard to develop and will be completely developed in our twenties. Until then, it's a lot of regrettable piercings, speeding tickets, and unsuitable romantic partners.

We're smack in the middle of that growth. Almost four billion people—more than half the world's population—are connected, and it won't be long before we all are. Most people reading this will be alive when everyone in the world who wants to be connected online can be. Just imagine what will be possible when the collective power of all those diverse perspectives can come together online on single issues like the environment, equality, or scientific inquiry. We are just starting to get a glimpse of the potential, with one recent example being the visualization and confirmation of a black hole, made possible by the combined computing power of a diverse group of scientists.

However, to reach these kind of insights, we need strategies both individually and as a society. When I think back to the early days of the Web's formation in the '90s, when there were just millions online, what we envisioned as the potential of the Web was an open, decentralized way to connect people and ideas. We never imagined a planet of screen obsessives, everyone looking down instead of up. But perhaps this phase is part of the process, just like the brain goes through its different stages.

It's time to move on to the next phase of development. Because it won't be long before everyone will be online, with the potential to access all human knowledge, to facilitate cross-disciplinary thinking on a scale we've never seen. But along with the potential that comes with this leap for our species, we need to ask some extremely important and urgent questions.

How do we ensure that when the rest of the planet comes online we don't make the same mistakes? How do we create frameworks that allow new users to make good decisions, to develop in a way that's healthy and sustainable? How do we create and use the Web more intentionally, so that we can nurture, grow, and prune it to reach its potential? How can we change *our* behaviors so that the Web better serves us?

I believe that Tech Shabbat is part of the solution. Living 24/6 works as the prefrontal cortex does: it forces you to stop what you're doing, examine your circumstances, slow down, and focus on what's important. To think before you act.

Right now we've got this big, brand-new set of tools, and we haven't figured out how to live with them yet. It's like we are pushing all the buttons on a fancy new car that moves in all directions, and we don't really understand how to drive in a safe way. We're not even sure we're on the right road. We are going way too fast, and we're texting at the wheel.

It's time to turn things around. If enough people start unplugging on a regular basis, we can start to strengthen our society's cultural prefrontal cortex. This doesn't mean thinking as one entity, but rather reinstating a collective cultural practice that inspires not only more long-term thinking but also more appreciation of the simple joys of life.

We can use 24/6 living and the skills it develops to work toward the future we want. While the Internet can be an exhilarating idea accelerator, creating an atmosphere of thoughts, theories, and opinions colliding and generating new ones at the speed of light, we also need to hold a much bigger mental space to process and assess all that is happening. How do we create a society that brings back this type of reflection? We need it. We need a new mode to turn it *all* off: not just airplane mode, but Shabbat mode, present mode, delight mode, daydreaming mode, deep and long-term-thinking mode, peaceful mode, connection mode, and reflection mode.

Let's evolve how we think, live, and work. We have to start viewing rest as a strength, not a weakness, and reward people for taking care of their bodies and minds, as well as creating infrastructures that support this across socioeconomic strata. We need to create more opportunities to bring people together, face-to-face, without screens, and we have to offer time and space for that to happen. Because the alternative is living as though technology invented us to serve its needs rather than the other way around.

Change can begin with some basic concrete steps.

Unplugging once a week is a foundational one. But it doesn't end there. In the workplace, we need to create work schedules that return and protect employees' time off and away from screens.

University of California Berkeley philosophy professor John Campbell writes, "Philosophy is thinking in slow motion." We can be hopeful that we are slowing down some thinking around the consequences of tech with the launching of some new initiatives that will ideally better guide where we are going. In Australia, a new branch of engineering is being established by the cultural anthropologist and futurist Genevieve Bell at the 3A Institute to explore the ethics of what we're creating. And in the United States, a consortium of twenty-one universities called the Public Interest Technology University Network formed in 2019 with the twofold goal of training technologists (like computer engineers) to focus on human concerns, and humanists (like social policymakers) to consider technological ones. Silicon Valley insiders backed the founding of the Center for Humane Technology, which is working to align technology's goals with those of humankind. And the new Unintended Consequences of Technology conference convenes annually to examine where we are, where we're going, and where we want to be.

We can raise the next generation differently. Let's wait until eighth grade to give children smartphones (and give them simpler phones a couple years before that if we need to). Let's create more devices that let us stay in touch with one another without giving ourselves access to everything all the time, distracting us from the people and things around us. Let's put phones away at work and at home, set more boundaries, and monitor screen time all around. Let's take time to unplug with friends, partners, parents, and kids, and create weekly practices, whether you call them Tech Shabbat or living 24/6 or something else.

We all have a profound need for stillness, silence, a day of reflection away from the noise. We are not designed to be stimulated all the time, nor do we want to be. Letting your mind have back its most reflective mode lets you see the best way forward.

Years from now, our ever-evolving world will have evolved yet again, and there will be new and more invisible ways to be plugged into the network, but Tech Shabbat and living 24/6 will be even more important. We'll need Heschel's palace in time to ground and protect us as the future continues to rush toward us. And we'll also need to look up when we emerge from it.

21

Life Is (In)Finite

When my father chose his burial spot, he selected a hill with a flat rock headstone laid horizontal among the wildflowers. This incline slopes down to the coast, but he didn't want his grave to face the ocean, even though he loved the ocean. Instead, his view for eternity is the small enclave of houses with slanted roofs where we lived in the halcyon days when we were a young, intact family.

Sitting there every year, on the anniversary of his death, I think a lot about what's finite and what's infinite. People always told me, "Your father was larger than life." Which he definitely was. But since he is gone, he is with me in a million more ways. He is larger than death, too.

If constraints feed creativity, then the ultimate constraint of death inspires the most meaningful creativity of all. Knowing that we are only here for a short while liberates us to live fully and deeply. What makes life beautiful and precious is that it's finite. I know many people in the tech world who want to live forever. I never thought that would be a good thing. Living a good life ultimately means being conscious that it will end.

Life continues to speed up the older you get. But I also know that my tool to slow things down and to live life most fully is to turn things off. And when I reflect back on my favorite moments, when I really felt present and connected with the people in my life, I usually find that all those moments took place on Tech Shabbat, the day that feels limitless.

Which always brings me back to the thoughts of infinity that come when I visit my father's grave. If we focus on things that are infinite, I believe, we could live our lives more abundantly.

Like love: the more you love, the more love there is.

And memory: memories of the good moments in life grow and expand the more you create space to write and reflect about them.

Gratitude also feels boundless. The more I started focusing on noticing, calling out, and writing down what I appreciated, my sense of gratitude grew, and I now understand it to be an infinite power.

Creativity feels infinite if you can create discipline to nurture it. As Maya Angelou says: "You can't use up creativity. The more you use, the more you have."

Empathy seems to grow once you focus on it. If you spend the time to truly connect with others, or if you put yourself in situations to really try to understand what others are going through, you will strengthen your ability to relate to them.

Power feels infinite to me. Some people think power is finite, which is why they often strive to have such a strong grasp on it. But it does seem to me that the more power is shared, the more it expands, and the more we can change our world.

———

If you are lucky enough to live to the far end of the average life expectancy, you'll get eighty-two years. As I mentioned earlier, that's about thirty thousand days. There are a lot of ways you could spend those days. What do you want to do that you haven't done? What makes you happy? Who do you want to be more present for? What do you have to contribute to the world? What gives your life purpose? How do you want to spend your days?

Humans have been asking these questions for millennia. At times of great change, we as individuals and as a society need to rise to meet the new realities with new responses to these very old questions.

Today we're in a pivotal era, transitioning from an analog society to a digital one. It's a turbulent time, but an exciting one, as we connect people and knowledge on unprecedented levels. Once again, we need to step up and ask: *How do we adapt? What does a meaningful life look like in our changed and changing world?*

I'm going to continue living 24/6, and encourage others to do the same, because it's one of the most profound ways I've found to have the time and space to think about who I am, what I value, and what I can bring to the world. It has opened up a whole new way of thinking about everything, including love, death, and technology. While the 24/7 world makes us crave a type of "more" that can leave us feeling empty, stepping away from that once a week to look at who we are, and to consider what kind of world we want, will refuel and guide us as we go.

———

In my father's last months, I repeatedly asked him, what did he think was the meaning of life?

Here is what he eventually said to me: "Appreciate beauty.

Plant gardens. Enjoy sunsets. Help people less fortunate than you. Think big. Nothing is more important than family. Be present." Much later, I would realize these are exactly the things we do on our screen-free days.

I started doing Tech Shabbats after the intense period when I lost my father and had Blooma within days. It was as if life grabbed me by the shoulders and stared into my eyes and said, *Figure out what's important!*

Here's the thing that's most fascinating to me, nearly a decade after my father's death: he is now infinite to me. While we are all human, fallible, imperfect beings who are all works in progress, if we attempt to live meaningful and purposeful lives and are present for those we love, we can live forever.

Someone once told me: whenever you are doing something that the person you lost loved to do, you bring them back. So while I write this book in the darkness of five a.m., when my dad also loved to write; clap through tears at the end of a fantastic film in a packed theater; thrust my own finger in the air and say, "Tradition!" while eating a bagel, lox, and cream cheese; or appreciate the family sitting around the table—all things he loved—he is with me.

If I have the privilege of living long enough to see my hair turn gray, and if I experience the joy of having grandchildren that I can hold in my sun-spotted hands . . . and if on my final day, as my body is shutting down, I lose my ability to speak, with only my eye contact left, I would hope Ken; Odessa; Blooma; my brother, Jordan; sister, Kimberly; best friends; and grandchildren are all gathered around me, leaning into me, close enough to hear what my eyes are saying. Here's what they would try to convey:

More presence
More appreciating
More compassion
More laughing
More dancing
More making
More kneading dough
More mistakes
More *I'm sorry*
More *I forgive you*
More eye contact
More hugs
More daydreaming
More silence
More eating together at the table
More reading
More journaling
More taking a beat
More thinking in slow motion
More rituals
More nature
More getting lost
More rest and digest
More tend and befriend
More empathy
More joy
More authentic connecting
More looking up
More love.

PART VII:
IT'S EASIER THAN YOU THINK:
A STEP-BY-STEP GUIDE

In this section you'll find everything you need to create a 24/6 life that works for you. It starts with prompts to get you thinking about what you hope to get back into your life. Then you'll unpack any obstacles and plan your experience. This is followed by checklists to help you prepare for the actual day, and age-appropriate ideas for fun things to do during your time off screens (an interesting commentary on our times that we even need this reminder list). Next, you'll find guidelines to help you incorporate more balance with technology the other six days of the week. Finally, people who keep a day of rest or who've tried living 24/6 share their experiences of what's worked for them. I'm excited for you to find ways this life-changing practice can work for you.

Things to Think About

These prompts are designed to help you think about what your 24/6 life could bring, as well as assess your screen use right now and decide what you'd like to change.

WHAT BRINGS YOU JOY?

Think about all the (screen-free) activities you enjoy doing that you just don't do enough. (It's okay if doing nothing is at the top of that list.) Here are some ideas to get you started:

- Cook a big meal with family or friends
- Listen to—or play—music
- Go to a farmers market, have a picnic
- Play baseball, basketball, throw a Frisbee
- Paint, garden, sing, dance, bike, hike, fly a kite
- Play board games, cards, charades, do a puzzle
- Read, write in a journal, sit under a tree
- Visit the ocean—or a special place you love
- Explore part of your town or city you don't know well

- Volunteer
- Sleep in, take a nap
- Go to a library or bookstore
- Pick up a new skill, or work on an old one
- Take a music lesson
- Start a family book club and discuss what you've read together each week
- Whatever brings you joy

CONSIDER YOUR OWN TRADITION OR HISTORY

- What foods or practices from your childhood, family, faith, or culture would make the day more meaningful for you?

CONSIDER YOUR INTENTIONS

- What qualities do you want to develop?
  - Empathy, patience, creativity, curiosity, self-control, humor, optimism, gratitude?
- What habits do you want to break?
- How do you want to feel when the day is over?

IDENTIFY THE BARRIERS

- What are your (or your partner's or kids') habits around screens that you most struggle with?
  - Checking the phone first thing in the morning
  - Checking the phone as a default any time you are waiting or not doing something else

- o Watching TV routinely or turning it on for background noise
  - o Too much time on social media
  - o Feeling disconnected from family members who are always on their phones
  - o Fear of missing out (FOMO)
  - o Becoming irritable when the screen is taken away
  - o Bringing laptop or smartphone into bed
- What's going to be the hardest part about giving up screens for a full day?
- What, if anything, do you fear will happen (or not happen)?
- Are you ready for this?

CHECK IN ON YOUR CURRENT SCREEN USE AND TIME ONLINE

- How many screens do you have in your house?
- How often do you think you're on at least one screen every day? Every week? Consider actually tracking your screen time, either with an app on your phone, on a spreadsheet, or through nondigital means.
- What aspects of your screen use worry you?
- When is the first time you check your phone in the morning?
- What is the longest amount of time you can remember being away from at least one screen?
- When was the last time you went a whole day without screens?

FOCUS ON THE BIGGER PICTURE

- How is unplugging regularly good for society? How can you be part of this process?
- How has your concept of "rest" changed throughout your life? Is it something that you want more or less than you used to?
- Think about how you want to be remembered, and start living that life.

HOW TO PREPARE FOR 24/6

A little thinking ahead will help you get more out of the day.

PLAN YOUR FIRST TECH SHABBAT

- Look at your calendar and determine what weekend day (or weekday) you're going to start. Mark down several weeks in a row. The power and beauty of this practice come with its regularity. In time you will look forward to it each week.
- Look at the list of things you want to do more of. Plan to fill your screen-free day with activities from that list. You can even print the list, post it on your fridge, and reference it throughout the day. Or fill the day with doing nothing, if that's what you need and want.
- Invite anyone you want to join you for a meal, an activity, or the whole day.
- Print out phone numbers (key friends, family, and emergency phone numbers) or other important information you may typically look up on your phone.
- Print any maps you may need to travel to a new place.

THINGS TO THINK ABOUT

- Get a landline. You can get one for as little as $20 a month.
- Tell people in your life (family, friends, coworkers, boss) you're planning to do this. Don't come from a place of apology, but a place of strength and excitement. If they express concern or curiosity, invite them to a Tech Shabbat dinner so they can experience it with you.

REFLECT ON YOUR FIRST TECH SHABBAT AND MAKE ADJUSTMENTS

- What was your experience like? How did it feel?
- Did you notice any physical, emotional, or mental changes? What were they?
- What worked for you?
- What was the hardest part?
- What was the best part?
- What, if anything, surprised you?
- What would you change for next time?
- Is there anyone else you want to bring along next time?
- How will you use screens differently this week?

Ideas for Having Fun without Screens (By Age)

For the most part, a whole day of unstructured time is wonderful. But for some people—especially littler ones—you need to be ready with a list of activities. Actually, for all ages, it's good to be reminded of all the fantastic things there are to do that don't involve screens or being online. Here are some age-appropriate ideas to keep the day interesting, all suggested by people in those age groups.

AGES 5 AND UNDER

- Read: Few activities are better for kids' cognitive development—and your bonding with them—than reading to them. Read old favorites or go to the library and stock up on new ones. Let them help pick out the stories.
- Write: Have the children dictate a story to you. When it's done, they can illustrate it. They can draw a self-portrait and dictate an "About the Author" page for the back.
- Imaginative play: There are countless options here—

school, store, family, restaurant, castle, magicians, robots. Costumes and accessories can make this even more fun.

- Play games: Board games, card games, and puzzles. You could even try inventing your own games.
- Cook: Put out a bunch of ingredients (e.g., chopped fruits and vegetables, yogurt, hummus, peanut butter, pretzels, crackers) and let the kids combine them to invent new dishes.
- Craft: Paint, sculpt, color, draw. Try big art projects, like life-size self-portraits on butcher paper, or smaller ones that use household items like paper towel rolls, paper clips, cotton balls, cotton swabs, bottle caps, etc.
- Nature: Go outside. Take a walk or look for interesting bugs and plants.
- Get physical: Do yoga, stretch, dance, run, play tag, play with a ball.
- Music: Sing, play an instrument, improvise percussion instruments (spoons, pots, pans, the floor, etc.), or just listen to your favorite songs and have a dance party.
- Build: Pillow forts and obstacle courses are especially fun.
- Hide: Play hide-and-seek or hide little treasures for the kids to find.
- Perform: Encourage the kids to put on a performance for you.
- Animals: Visit an animal shelter or a dog park.

AGES 6 TO 12

- Read: Any printed material counts, even comic books. At this age, they're old enough to read alone, but it can still be fun and gratifying to read together.

- Write: Journal. Write a story or poem, or make a newspaper for the family or the neighborhood. Write a real letter and mail it.
- Search: Let the kids create a treasure hunt, complete with cryptic clues.
- Upcycle: Turn recycling materials into structures, like a fort or a clubhouse.
- Invent: Encourage them to make a prototype of their ideas (brilliant or otherwise).
- Music: Practice the instrument they already play or learn a new one. They can even try creating their own.
- Nature: Go for a hike—have them dial into the sounds they hear, the scents they smell, and new things they see.
- Set up shop: Open a lemonade stand or other pop-up.
- Play games: Board games, card games, and puzzles. Or find some cardboard and design your own board game.
- Dress up: Someone picks a profession (doctor, rock star, librarian) and the other person or people have to go into closets and create that look.
- Wordplay: Try learning some phrases in a new language, or even inventing their own.
- Perform: Write and perform a play or musical. If the kids are really missing TV, have them write and perform their own TV show.
- Craft: Paint, sculpt, color, draw. Make jewelry, knit, or crochet. If you don't know how, you can all learn together.
- Cook: Make something to enjoy together, or provide ingredients for an *Iron Chef*–style cooking challenge.
- Get physical: Do yoga, dance, run, ride bikes. Play soccer or basketball.

- Volunteer: Helping other people is a wonderful way to spend screen-free time.

AGES 13 TO 17

- Sleep in!
- If you play an instrument, invite friends or family to play music with you. If you don't, and you want to learn, it's a great day to start.
- Read for fun.
- Write for fun. Journal. If you get stuck, you can use these prompts:
    - Write a list of things you are grateful for.
    - Write a list of qualities you like about yourself and things you want to work on.
- Hike, bike, picnic, spend time outdoors.
- Cook a big meal with family, or bake something sweet and share it with friends or neighbors.
- Go for a walk around the neighborhood.
- Do a scavenger hunt with friends.
- Plant something.
- Play soccer, baseball, basketball, Frisbee, or tennis.
- Skate, skateboard, ride a scooter, or rollerblade.
- Paint, draw, or sculpt. Make a portrait, a self-portrait, or a still life.
- Sing. Dance.
- Meditate.
- Volunteer at a senior center.
- Go through books you want to donate or give to friends.
- Go to the library or an independent bookstore.

- Play board games or cards. Do a giant puzzle.
- Visit a body of water. Pools count.

AGES 18+

- Cook a big meal with family or friends.
- Bake something for someone else.
- Get some fresh air. Go for a walk around the neighborhood or a long walk in nature.
- Write for pleasure. Journal. Try out these prompts:
  - Write a list of things you're grateful for.
  - Write a list of what you appreciate about your partner or friend.
  - Write a list of qualities you like about yourself and things you want to work on.
  - Write down things you are excited about, things you are worried about, and things you may have worried about that never came to fruition.
- Write a thank-you note or letter to a friend, teacher, or mentor.
- Send a friend a favorite book.
- Pay attention to little moments of beauty and write about them.
- Tell your parents something valuable they have taught you.
- Unplug all appliances that aren't being used.
- Listen to or play music or just sing. Take up a new instrument.
- Dance!
- Have a picnic.
- Play baseball, basketball, tennis, throw a Frisbee.

- Paint, draw, sculpt, or watercolor.
- Visit an art museum.
- Go to the library or an independent bookstore.
- Go through books you want to donate or give to friends.
- Take a bike ride.
- Fly a kite.
- Play board games, cards, puzzles, charades. Host a game night or a trivia challenge.
- Read for pleasure.
- Read or write a poem.
- Think of your favorite words and teach them to a child in your life.
- Think of a fun memory with a sibling or cousin and write it in a note to send.
- Use a landline to call someone you miss.
- Visit a community garden, or if you have one of your own, plant something.
- Visit a nearby body of water and go swimming.
- Take a long bath or shower.
- Meditate.
- Do yoga or just stretch.
- Take a nap.

AGES 65+

- Make plans: Is there an art show you want to see? Is there a part of town you want to visit? A friend you'd like to catch up with?
- Start with dinner: Potluck, or cook together, or go to a restaurant you've been wanting to try or already love.

- Play cards: Start a weekly card game.
- Volunteer: Shelters and hospitals always need helping hands.
- Reminisce: Visit with a different friend each week to share old memories together. Get out the photo albums.
- Make a project: Spend Tech Shabbat afternoons putting together the story of your life for posterity, in words, pictures, or both.
- Exercise: Swim, take a walk, go to a yoga class.
- Family time: Plan screen-free activities with the family (especially grandchildren, if you have any—see lists on pages 185–91 for ideas).

Keep the Physical and Mental Benefits Going the Other Six Days of the Week

SCREEN USE

- Establish guidelines for where and when screens can be used (like no phones on the table during meals).
- Put a small notebook in your bag, with a pen that you love, and consider a paper scheduler. This way, you'll pull out this book instead of your phone any moment you want to jot something down, schedule something, or record something. You can even get one the size of a phone if it'll make you feel more comfortable.
- Use the feature that's now on smartphones to set limits on screen use or social media use.
- Set a text auto-response from your phone when you go offline so that people know you're unavailable. And let them know you are enjoying life away from the screen. For example, "I have my phone off to rebalance my mind. Will write to you when I am back refreshed."

- Set aside time each day to let your mind wander: while taking a shower, doing the dishes, driving, walking, biking, exercising. Try not to fill those times with talking on the phone or listening to podcasts or news.
- Wait until eighth grade (WaitUntil8th.org) to get kids a smartphone.
- If your child needs a phone before then, consider getting a simple model, like a flip phone with limited or no Internet access.
- Check out smartphone contracts for your kids by Janell Burley Hofmann (janellburleyhofmann.com/the-contract/) or Dr. Delaney Ruston (screenagersmovie.com/contracts/).
- Revisit the contract every six months or as new developments, needs, and interests evolve.
- More websites and organizations can be found at the resources section on page 219.

REST, SILENCE, AND STILLNESS

- Get an old-fashioned alarm clock for your room so you don't need a phone to wake you up.
- Don't look at screens for at least thirty minutes after you wake up. Try journaling instead.
- Establish periods of quiet rest throughout the day—leave the phone behind and go take a walk, go outside for lunch, practice a musical instrument or take up an easy one, like the ukulele, or write in a journal instead of scrolling on your phone. Create space to let your mind wander. Two hours a day of silence is recommended.

- Make a list of all your favorite places in nature that are close to where you live that you want to visit more.
- Go somewhere without Wi-Fi for the day or longer.
- Don't let screens be the last thing you do before you sleep. The blue light can interfere with sleep onset. Read a book or a magazine instead.

EXITS AND ENTRANCES

- Start paying attention to what you're doing when you arrive at or leave a space.
- Finish calls before you enter a room.
- Try the thirty-second hug (see pages 83–84).
- Try the ten-second doorknob countdown (see page 84).
- Before texting someone, remember it takes twenty-three minutes to return to focus after each interruption. Is the text really that urgent? Could it be emailed so they can choose when to look at it?
- With kids, practice "the entrance" of how to answer the landline: "Hello, XY residence."

EMPATHY AND EYE CONTACT

- Make eye contact and say hello, good morning, etc., to five new people every day.
- Get to know the names of people you interact with regularly but whose name you may not know—at work, at your favorite cafe, at the library, in the neighborhood, at school drop-off or pickup.

- Forgive someone.
- Give people the benefit of the doubt.
- Write a list of people you would like to get to know better and why. Invite them to your next Tech Shabbat meal.

SOCIAL MEDIA USE

- Turn off all social media and app notifications on your phone so it's not constantly asking for your attention. You choose when to check in.
- Adopt a social media strategy. Ask yourself, *Why am I on social media right now? Is it for work or school? For news? Is it to connect with family and friends? Who am I following and why?* Remember, your feeds are shaping your thoughts and your mind.
- Take a beat before posting. Is what you're about to post authentic? Are your posts showing only one version of yourself? How will people receive it? Is it something you want to broadcast to everyone who follows you? Is this information best communicated face-to-face with close friends and family, or on a call, or in an email or text?
- Take a social media sabbatical. Taking an occasional week off can be great for your schedule as well as your soul. Take stock of how you feel afterward.

WORK/SCHOOL AND PRODUCTIVITY

- Talk with coworkers or peers about keeping phones out of sight (not on desks if in a shared space)—especially during meetings; just having smartphones out distracts everyone in the room.

- When working solo or at home, put the phone away while you are trying to focus.
- Take a beat before responding to an email that upsets you. Sleep on it.
- Try tech tools designed to keep you more focused, such as OneTab, which condenses all your open tabs, or Momento, which asks you when you open your browser, "What's your main priority for today?" A full list of updated resources can be found at 24SixLife.com.
- Educators and parents: Consider visiting AwayForThe Day.org, an initiative that supports parents and schools in limiting smartphones in schools.

GRATITUDE

- Keep a stack of thank-you notes and stamps in your bag so you can write and send one any time you think about it.
- Write a letter of appreciation and send it to a friend, teacher, or mentor.
- Keep a gratitude notepad with you so you can reach for that instead of your phone when you are waiting some-where.
- Start *The Five-Minute Journal* or an appreciation journal (see page 138).
- If you have a hard time going to sleep at night, think of three things you are grateful for when you close your eyes.

Everything (But the Screen) Challah Recipe

The first few times we attempted to make challah, we produced a brown, hard rock. When people bit into it, they smiled wanly and mumbled, "It is the best one yet." "Yet" is the key word there. Slowly, there was change. The challahs became fluffy, and "hmms" became "mmms." Here's our formula, adapted from one of my best friends Julie Hermelin's "One Mighty Fine Challah" recipe.

INGREDIENTS

For Bread
1 cup hot water (95–105 degrees)
3 packets Fleischmann's fast-acting yeast
⅓ cup sugar
½ tbsp salt
3½ cups of flour (plus more for kneading)
1 egg

¼ cup canola oil

   (plus 2 to 3 tablespoons for greasing the bowl)

oil spray (for greasing the pan)

For Topping

1 egg

Everything-bagel-seed topping (otherwise known as "Tornado Dust."
   You can order it from the Great Barrington Bagel Company, or buy
   the Trader Joe's version. You can also make it yourself from poppy
   seeds, sesame seeds, toasted garlic, and kosher salt.)

1. Make the dough in the morning so the challah has all day
   to rise. Combine 1 cup hot water (hot, but not so hot as to
   burn you or kill the yeast) with three packages of fast-rising
   yeast (I finally learned it's three packages and not just one).
   Add ⅓ cup sugar and ½ tablespoon salt into the bowl and
   mix together. Let the yeast mixture sit for at least 30 minutes
   until it gets activated.

2. Add 2 cups flour. This is a great time to taste the dough
   (before the raw egg is added).

3. In a separate bowl, beat together one egg and ¼ cup canola
   oil. Then stir this into the flour mixture. Slowly add the
   remaining 1½ cups of flour.

4. Sprinkle some flour on the counter and then dump the
   dough onto it. Flour your hands so the dough won't stick to
   them, and knead away. Push, pull, knead, fold the dough on
   itself, and repeat. The feeling of dough between your fingers

and flour being mixed together on Friday mornings is truly one of life's great pleasures.

We somethimes sing the following song as we knead the challah: "Challah, challah, challah, watch it rise! Push your love into it, way up high!" (Once Odessa and Blooma were fighting when we were kneading the challah, and some anger was pushed into that challah, too, and it turned out to be our fluffiest one ever. Lots of hot air is apparently also good to make it rise.)

5. Grease bowl with 2–3 tablespoons of canola oil. Put dough back in, and cover with a damp towel. Allow to sit and rise for the rest of the day.

6. When you are ready to bake the challah, preheat oven to 350 degrees. Then, divide the fluffy risen dough into three separate balls. With your hands, roll out each of the three separate balls into a medium-length ropelike strand. Braid the strands together, then place on a baking sheet coated with cooking spray.

7. In a separate bowl, beat one egg. Brush the top of the challah with the egg for a lovely glaze effect. Then add the "every-thing" on top.

8. Slide that loaf of love in the oven. Bake for about 25 or 30 minutes. To test for doneness, gently poke the challah. It should give a bit but shouldn't be too doughy.

9. Remove from the oven and let cool a bit. We like to serve it by tearing off a piece and sharing it to the person next to you.

People Share Their Perspectives on Living 24/6, Tech Shabbat, and Shabbat

Living 24/6 can work for anyone, from any background, and there's no one right way to do it. Here's what it looks like for many different people, from many different backgrounds: some who do Tech Shabbat regularly, some who observe a more traditional Shabbat, and some who are trying it for the first time.

If you'd like to share your own experience, or read more inspiration from others along with films and resources, please go to 24SixLife.com.

Amy Emmerich (Refinery29 president and chief content officer); Colin Oberschmidt (motion picture studio technician); Emzy, 6; Flash, 4

1. Why did you want to try unplugging?
We wanted to show our kids that tech isn't the most important thing, while connecting more deeply with them.

2. Describe your Tech Shabbat experience.

Doing Tech Shabbat was awesome. We loved it. My husband and I were away from the kids most of Saturday, and we loved having the time together, fully focused on each other, actually making eye contact when speaking. We both realized how addicted we are to our phones as we kept going to grab them. Fundamentally shutting them down MUST happen or you would cheat. With the kids, LEGOs and Play-Doh were the star toys for time (five hours) and imagination. We made a ton of Play-Doh food and opened a restaurant, creating menus and eating and being served in the restaurant. It was awesome to see the kids' minds open up.

3. What was most difficult for you?

We don't have a landline, so that was tough. We didn't wear watches, and it proved beneficial as it caused us to interact more with strangers. Asking, "Hey, what time do you have?" felt a bit nostalgic, but it worked every time. Getting a car is an issue in New York. It's all about Ubers, Lyfts, and our phones. We only put one phone on and truly watched each other only call a car then shut it off. We have to figure out a way around that.

Another party foul was Alexa. The kids started using it in the mornings for music. We addressed it and started using the record player. We had many conversations around music. We realized Alexa makes listening easy, but there is no discussion over "What do you want to listen to?" as you just yell it out. Records required us to have meaningful discussions around artists.

4. What surprised you the most?

How much we enjoyed one another and the fun we had.

5. What is your biggest takeaway?
That it really isn't painful! LOVE THIS TECH SHABBAT—we are addicted.

Martin Rozenblum (founder of Visibility.org)

1. Why do you keep Shabbat?
During the week I'm a hyperconnected person and, to my own surprise, slowly came to the enjoyment and understanding of Shabbat. I tested every possible iteration of the Shabbat experience for at least two years. I experienced driving, being driven, or not traveling at all, accepting phone calls, just texting or having the phone off, leaving the TV on or not, etcetera. . . . I tried different variations to see what felt right to me. There is a balance that each one of us can find appropriate to our place in life. However, the experience under absolute disconnection is magically rewarding beyond others.

2. Describe your typical Shabbat experience in regard to screens. What do you do?
I sleep around fourteen hours and recover from a hectic week. It feels like the deepest vacation, no matter where in the world I am. The day is only about being present, not worried about what's happening anywhere else, but where I am and what I'm about to do. It's a day of focused meditation concentrated on doing the things that are good for me. The rabbinical sages also indicate that all the blessings of the week come to you on Shabbat, so why lose such an opportunity to enjoy them?

3. What is most difficult for you about unplugging from screens one day a week?
To make friends and family understand that they can't reach me for twenty-four hours, unless they want to come by to say hello. There is nothing new about this—it's just old-school. I don't understand why everyone has such an issue with it. . . .

4. What surprises you the most about unplugging one day a week?
Why aren't more people experiencing it?

5. What is your biggest takeaway from keeping a screen-free Shabbat?
Health!

Haim Goldberg (mentalist, TV personality, inventor); Miriam Goldberg (manager, producer); Adir, 12; Mia, 10

1. Why did you want to try this?
Sounded like a fun experiment—and we are collectively complaining that we are on our phones too much.

2. Describe your Tech Shabbat experience.
We are a very active family and very close. We do a lot of family activities on a regular basis, and there is rarely a weekend where we don't do something. But on Tech Shabbat, we've been more in the moment, more present. When we were out and saw other families, we noticed the whole family was on the phone, while our family was talking to each other. We managed to do so much more, and I realized the reason I managed to do so much was because

I wasn't on my phone. It's like going to the dollar store—you pick up an item here and an item there and in the end it's $100. It's the same with the phone. You go five minutes here, five minutes there, mindlessly, from Facebook to Instagram. It's not purposeful use; it's mindless browsing, and suddenly you lose an hour or two.

3. What was most difficult for you?
Taking away the comfort of all the helper apps like GPS, Clock, and WhatsApp, since my family lives overseas and we communicate via the Internet.

4. What surprised you the most?
For me, how much extra time we have without our phones. For my husband, Haim, that he actually can fall asleep without his phone. The experiment (and me) made him put away his phone before bedtime—the result was that he had the best sleep that he's had in years.

5. What is your biggest takeaway?
The reason we want to continue doing it is we got such positive feedback from the kids. The whole day, they mentioned how much they were loving it—they felt that we were truly present. Of course, we all went on our electronics at six p.m., but I think we all would benefit from another half a day at least. Our son, Adir, said, "It was really fun. I didn't miss my phone that much. I think it's just good to take a break from my phone, to spend more time with family." And our daughter, Mia, said, "I feel like we had way more time. I always feel like I have no time when I have my phone. I want to do it 24/5!"

We are even thinking of taking breaks during the week. We

got a little more aware, looking at the time management function.
I think that this Tech Shabbat thing is a keeper. . . .

Daniel Goldin (former chief administrator of NASA, 1992–2001; president and CEO of KnuEdge)

1. Why did you want to try this?
Tiffany [Shlain] told me so much about how a screen-free day
provided relief from the connected life and enhanced the family
connectivity, my wife and I decided to try.

2. Describe your screen-free day experience.
We spent the restful disconnected day with my cousins who were
visiting from back east and also engaged other friends from LA.

3. What was most difficult for you?
No withdrawal symptoms or driving need to text.

4. What surprised you the most about unplugging?
No big deal, we weren't in a life-and-death situation. We were taking time to enjoy friends and family and just disconnected elec-
tronically.

5. What is your biggest takeaway from unplugging one day a week?
Enjoyment with family and friends. It has been the most amazing
feeling. It's not just work I feel I have to be available for 24/7—but
it's personal, it's children, friends. I just feel like I have so many
obligations. For one day to be off any screen with my wife felt terrific. I got to clear my mind.

Vincent DeLuca (filmmaker)

1. Why do you keep Shabbat?

I have a good friend who went to divinity school at Duke; today, he's a pastor in Toronto. I ended up going to law school with him. He got into old-school theology. We started to practice Shabbat in graduate school. I've been practicing Shabbat for fifteen years. I'm a Christian. I think of Shabbat as a Jewish practice, and there is some real truth and wisdom there—some deep wisdom on how we should be living.

2. Describe your typical Shabbat experience in regard to screens. What do you do?

My life gets crazy. Shabbat is a great time to be grounded. I try to go out and do things in nature. I try to disconnect from email and not do anything work related. I had to tell my film partner. When I didn't respond to some messages, he wrote, "Are you okay?" "Yes, dude. I took Saturday off."

3. What is most difficult for you about unplugging from screens one day a week?

I think I have FOMO. There's almost a magnet pull that is calling me to look at my phone or check emails in case there is a crisis happening or an issue that needs addressing.

4. What surprises you the most about unplugging one day a week?

How good it feels. I've been reading John O'Donohue's book *Beauty: The Invisible Embrace*, in which he talks about true inner beauty versus the artificial glamour that pops up as what we normally take for beauty. These two principles—beauty and glamour—have opposite effects on us. Beauty pulls us to deep, long-lasting truths, while glamour shines for only so long. I think Shabbat shifts our attention away from glamour to beauty, allowing us to move into a contemplative space that nourishes our souls.

5. What is your biggest takeaway from keeping a screen-free Shabbat?

Throughout the week, I am a better version of myself when I keep Shabbat. My heart and mind are refreshed, and this manifests in my behavior. This is important not just for my own well-being but for everyone I come into contact with.

Jenn Lee Smith (film producer and writer); Lund Smith (COO of WSJ Properties); Kaelyn, 12; Devyn, 9; Jake, 7

1. Why did you want to try this?

Reducing screen time in the home continues to be a frequent topic of conversation for us. Lund and I grew up with the television as the only screen presence in our daily lives. When our children were young, we reflected on how they will never know a world without digital screens. It didn't take long to arrive at the decision that we must take an active role in unplugging, as screen products are cleverly designed to keep the human mind (however small) craving and wanting more. If we didn't purposefully set boundaries, the result would be less quality and connective time with one another. Through trial and error we landed on one room in the house as the place for usage. But there were no hard-and-fast rules on *when* tech could be used. When I first heard of Tech Shabbat, I knew we needed to incorporate the practice into our family life.

2. Describe your Tech Shabbat experience.

Our third attempt at Tech Shabbat: We said a blessing over food on Friday night and broke bread with family visiting from Indiana. Saturday morning was spent playing tennis and Ping-Pong, followed by a review of schoolwork for the week and quiet reading time. Then lunch with family, then our nine-year-old daughter, Devyn, had two basketball games. We didn't need digital maps to guide us anywhere. I knew our seven-year-old, Jake, would have a hard time unplugging, so earlier in the week we had checked out more books than normal from the library. Besides reading, Jake joined his sister in puzzles, so, success! He was able to occupy himself without an iPad. We noticed a slight behavior change in the evening from the two little ones. Normally, when we go out on a date, they stand by the door and peg us with questions about where we're going and when we'll return. That night, they seemed less antsy and more content in general.

3. What was most difficult for you?

I've become so dependent on my smartphone for calendaring my life, navigation, and communication that I ended up relying on the device during the first two attempts at Tech Shabbat for all of those things. Even though I did prepare, some last-minute engagements screwed up all my best intentions.

4. What surprised you the most?

We finally decided to plan fewer activities leading up to and during Tech Shabbat. It was nice to end the evening earlier. During the day, however, it felt strange to not be actively going somewhere or doing something. But as the day progressed I felt a genuine appreciation for a slower tempo. The children remarked, too, how much they like not having so many activities. One said, "I like being bored."

5. What is your biggest takeaway?

We're going to be adopting many if not all of these rituals for a long time and modifying and adapting as our family needs change over time. Doing it is absolutely in line with what we believe at home and in our religion. Our church encouraged us to do a ten-day social media fast several months ago, which isn't exactly like a tech fast, but it's moving in that direction. We created rules around certain rooms being off-limits to devices. Tech Shabbat helped us to further limit usage on the weekends and helped us spend more meaningful time as a family.

Alan Eyzaguirre (product marketing and communications)

1. Why did you want to try this?

Life balance; work balance; stress management.

2. Describe your Tech Shabbat experience.

The great part about Tech Shabbat is that it is an antidote to creative writer's block. In today's tech-oriented world, the terms of competition are measured in creativity and output. But most of that content is created on a laptop or device. The tough part is, most people lose perspective when they are working relentlessly on a computer. The beauty of Tech Shabbat is that some of the best ideas percolate in the background of the mind, and to fuel that, one needs silence. Tech Shabbat inspires me over and over again.

3. What was most difficult for you?
Realizing how much I am dependent on technology.

4. What surprised you the most?
That I found myself longing for Friday night—like running a marathon every week. It was rewarding to calm the mind.

5. What is your biggest takeaway?
What I found is that I've intuitively gravitated toward Tech Shabbat practice as a way to nurture my own creativity—and going screen-free makes me feel connected to the historical and the present community supporting this ideal. Tech Shabbat truly inspired me to preserve a day of rest to ensure my vitality and connection to the world.

Farai Chideya (author and journalist; Ford Foundation journalism program officer)

1. Why did you want to try this?
I am someone who easily falls into the rabbit hole of checking my devices constantly. Part of it is my current job as a grantmaker, where I am doing everything on computer or phone except face-to-face meetings. I can justify some of this, but there's plenty of time when I can unplug if I put my mind to it.

2. Describe your Tech Shabbat experience.
I decided to do my Tech Shabbat six p.m. to six p.m. I had not made a plan for the Tech Shabbat as much as I had made an un-plan, paring down my schedule and obligations. I made a deli-

cious pot of soup and decided to rearrange the furniture in my living room. It is relatively spacious, but I had a cramped layout. Over the course of the evening I moved a few things around and got a great effect. I thought about the huge knot in my right shoulder from texting too much. . . . It was nice to give my body a break. I did take some notes in longhand on a writing project. The rest of the day went great. I felt much more able to tackle big things (like rethinking my living room) and much less harried.

3. What was most difficult for you?

I didn't complete Tech Shabbat two of three times I tried in a row, because I hadn't really aligned my life, and I had travel. The travel was a killer. Even things like how reliant we have become on Lyft and Uber struck me. For example, I was traveling for business to a location that required flying into SFO, spending a night, then going to Sonoma. If I was not to use a device it would have required booking the car travel well in advance.

4. What surprised you the most?

I really felt able to have some quiet time with myself and my own thoughts, and to also be playful and focused. I feel strongly that I can be more mindful and creative by doing Tech Shabbat. I definitely want to work it back into my life as a running experiment if not a way of life.

5. What is your biggest takeaway?

I think for me the key is to start out by doing some weeks that are easy layups—not travel days or days with variable schedules. It did make me feel much more centered and able to think in broader terms.

Dorthe Eisele (physicist and assistant professor of chemistry, City College of New York at CUNY)

1. Why do you keep Shabbat?
When we think about Shabbat, very often we think of rules and restrictions. And that makes it difficult to actually observe Shabbat. We need to understand that that's not the concept of Shabbat, to restrict us. The concept is to enjoy ourselves, to have a chance to reconnect with ourselves and what is larger than ourselves. The rules are made for the people, not the people for the rules. So whatever is a delight and joy for you and helps you to reconnect with yourself and your loved ones, you should do.

2. Describe your typical Shabbat experience.
On Shabbat morning, I can go for this very long run. I don't look at the time. I'm not trying to be competitive. It brings me so much joy.

3. What is your biggest takeaway?
Life is about joy. In my research group, we have this little saying: Enjoy the ride! Follow your interests, follow your joy.

Roy Hessel (founder and CEO, EyeBuyDirect, and CEO, Clearly.ca and Coastal.com)

1. Why do you keep Shabbat?
First and foremost, I keep Shabbat because as an observant Jew I have a requirement to do so. However, over the years the motivation to keep Shabbat has far surpassed the need to fulfill the

requirement, as it's driven by the pleasure of indispensable personal freedom, and uninterrupted family and community time. I cannot imagine life without Shabbat.

2. Describe your typical Shabbat experience in regard to screens. What do you do?

No screens, no work, no money, no travel. Instead, we invest our time in conversations, storytelling, reading, board games, and hosting family and friends.

3. What is most difficult for you about unplugging from screens one day a week?

Personally, there is no difficulty, I look forward to unplugging for twenty-five hours.* For our four children, however, it's slightly more difficult, so an hour before Shabbat often tends to involve some negotiations. . . .

4. What surprises you the most about unplugging one day a week?

In the absence of devices, I am always surprised by how easy it is to disconnect, how my clarity of thought and creativity improves, and how much better I sleep.

5. What is your biggest takeaway from keeping a screen-free Shabbat?

It's not enough to carve out time in your schedule. You need to approach this blackout period with an unwavering belief in its benefit and a commitment to see it through. For me, this means

---

* Orthodox Jews begin Shabbat a little before sunset and end it a little after, for a total of twenty-five hours.

abstaining from work and, in the deepest sense, simply resting. It grounds me and allows me to reenergize and focus on what's really important in my life.

The key is to be unapologetic rather than aspirational about unplugging. As soon as my family and I get home from our work-week, there's nothing, with the exception of a life-and-death situation, that would cause me to compromise that time. As far as business and my income is concerned, it can wait.

Casper ter Kuile (ministry innovation fellow, Harvard Divinity School)

1. Why did you start going offline one day a week?

I started in March 2014. I was browsing the library of Harvard Divinity School and came across Heschel's *The Sabbath*, which intrigued me. I grew up nonreligious so I wasn't quite sure what to expect, but I loved his language of the Sabbath being a "palace in time." I was studying and working part-time, so I felt the weeks flow into one another without a break and really wanted to create a ritual way of giving myself an intentional break now and then.

2. Describe your Tech Shabbat experience.

As it gets dark, I turn off my phone and laptop and hide them under a bookshelf. Then I light a candle and hold it in my hands as I sing a song I learned in summer camp in Holland. Translated, it means "Good night, oh beautiful sun, I give thanks for this day. In golden glory you descend, in our hearts you keep shining. Good night, oh beautiful sun, I give thanks for this day."

PEOPLE SHARE THEIR PERSPECTIVES

3. What is most difficult for you about unplugging one day a week?

There are three times that are really hard. The first is when it's time to stop, even though there are errands and work tasks that are not yet done. So as a little accountability tool I often post on social media before going offline, something like, *The work isn't finished, but it is time to stop. #techsabbath.*

The second is around three p.m. on a Saturday, when I'm itching to be productive or watch YouTube or check other social media.

Finally, if I am traveling, everything falls apart! I need Lyft or Google Maps or I'm navigating changing plans, so nearly always I end up breaking my Tech Shabbat.

4. What surprised you the most?

How transformative it is. My most creative ideas happen. I read more widely and deeply. And I have a nap on Saturday afternoon, which feels like the ultimate luxury.

Also, even though I live in a residence with twenty-eight freshmen, I've never had a single emergency where having my phone off was a problem.

5. What is your biggest takeaway?

It is now the foundation of my spiritual life. On the weeks when I miss it, I am much more likely to be cranky! I can't recommend it enough.

Resources

A full list of updated resources can be found at:
24SixLife.com.

Other resources:
AwayForTheDay.org
Center for Humane Technology (humanetech.com)
Center on Media and Child Health (cmch.tv)
CommonSenseMedia.org
DigitalWellnessCollective.com
Family Online Safety Institute (fosi.org)
NationalDayOfUnplugging.com
ScreenSense.org
WaitUntil8th.org

Related Filmography by the Author

All films can be viewed online with links at 24SixLife.com. You'll also find short films that were made specifically for *24/6*.

30,000 Days explores the three-thousand-year history of humans wrestling with the question of how to live life with meaning and purpose. (11 minutes)

Adaptable Mind underscores the importance of skills we need to thrive in the twenty-first century, like curiosity, creativity, taking initiative, multidisciplinary thinking, and empathy. (11 minutes)

Science of Character investigates the neuroscience and social science that proves that we can shape who we are and who we want to be in the world. (8 minutes)

Making of a Mensch travels back in history to look at ideas around developing one's character through the lens of the ancient Jewish teachings of Mussar. (10 minutes)

Brain Power uncovers the parallels between a child's brain development and the development of the global brain of Internet, and the best ways to shape both. (10 minutes)

Engage asks people around the world to put their hand on their heart and think about how they want to live. (2 minutes)

A Declaration of Interdependence is a rewriting of the Declaration of Independence to be a global Declaration of *Inter*dependence. Music by Moby. (4 minutes)

Facing the Future/The Friendship is a parody film about Facebook. (2 minutes)

Yelp: With Apologies to Allen Ginsberg's "Howl" lampoons the addictions of our generation. (3 minutes)

Connected: An Autoblogography about Love, Death, and Technology is a Sundance feature documentary that delves into Shlain's love/hate relationship with technology and serves as the springboard for an exploration of modern life . . . and our interconnected future. (80 minutes)

The Tribe is an unorthodox, unauthorized history of the Barbie doll and the Jewish people. By tracing the Barbie doll's history, the film asks: What does it mean to be an American Jew today? What does it mean to be a member of any tribe in the twenty-first century? (18 minutes)

The Future Starts Here (seasons 1 and 2), an Emmy-nominated series, explores what it means to be human in our increasingly connected world. Episodes relevant to the topics in this book are listed below and range from three to seven minutes long:

"Technology Shabbats"
"Motherhood Remixed"
Tech Etiquette"
"Why We Love Robots"
"Participatory Revolution"
"The Creative Process in 10 Acts"
"Idea Porn""
A Case for Optimism"
"A Case for Dreaming"
"Punk Rock Diplomacy"
"Robots, Botox, and Google Glass"
"The Photosynthesis of Social Media"
"TransBoom"
"ParenTechnology"
"Creative Bondage"
"The Future of Our Species"

Notes

1   Ana Levy-Lyons, "Sabbath Practice as Political Resistance:
     Building the Religious Counterculture," *Tikkun* 27, no. 5
     (2012): 16–67.

2   Press Release (Enterprise Rent-A-Car), "Work Invades the
     American Weekend: New Survey Reveals Almost Seven in
     10 Put in a Full Workday at Least One Weekend a Month"
     (April 26, 2017), https://www.enterpriseholdings.com
     /en/press-archive/2017/04/work_invades_the_american
     _weekend_survey.html.

3   Gloria Mark, Daniela Gudith, and Ulrich Klocke, "The
     Cost of Interrupted Work: More Speed and Stress," *Pro-
     ceedings of the SIGCHI Conference on Human Factors in
     Computing Systems* (Florence, Italy, April 5–10, 2008): 107–
     10, https://dl.acm.org/citation.cfm?doid=1357054.1357072.

4   Gideon P. Dunster, Luciano de la Iglesia, Miriam Ben-
     Hamo, Claire Nave, Jason G. Fleischer, Satchidananda

Panda, and O. Horacio, "Sleepmore in Seattle: Later School Start Times Are Associated with More Sleep and Better Performance in High School Students," *Science Advances* 4, no. 12 (2018): DOI: 10.1126/sciadv.aau6200.

5   Luisa De Vivo, Michele Bellesi, William Marshall, Eric A. Bushong, Mark H. Ellisman, Giulio Tononi, and Chiara Cirelli, "Ultrastructural Evidence for Synaptic Scaling across the Wake/Sleep Cycle," *Science* 355, no. 6324 (2017): 507–10.

6   Deirdre Barnett, *The Committee of Sleep*. (New York: Crown, 2001).

7   Larry Rosen, et al., "Sleeping with Technology: Cognitive, Affective, and Technology Usage Predictors of Sleep Problems among College Students," *Sleep Health* 2, no. 1 (2016): 49–56.

8   The Nielsen Company, "The Total Audience Report: QI 2016" (June 27, 2016), https://www.nielsen.com/us/en/insights/reports/2016/the-total-audience-report-q1-2016.html.

9   Holly B. Shakya and Nicholas A. Christakis, "Association of Facebook Use with Compromised Well-Being: A Longitudinal Study," *American Journal of Epidemiology* 185 (2017), 203–11.

10   Adrian F. Ward, Kristen Duke, Ayelet Gneezy, and Maarten W. Bos, "Brain Drain: The Mere Presence of One's Own

Smartphone Reduces Available Cognitive Capacity," *Journal of the Association for Consumer Research* 2, no. 2 (2017): 140–54.

11 Susan Dynarski, "Laptops Are Great, But Not During a Lecture or a Meeting," *New York Times* (November 22, 2017), https://www.nytimes.com/2017/11/22/business/laptops -not-during-lecture-or-meeting.html.

12 David D. Luxton, Jennifer D. June, and Jonathan M. Fairall, "Social Media and Suicide: A Public Health Perspective," *American Journal of Public Health* 102, no. S102 (2012): S195–S200.

13 Sara H. Konrath, Edward H. O'Brien, and Courtney Hsing, "Changes in Dispositional Empathy in American College Students over Time: A Meta-Analysis," *Personality and Social Psychology Review* 15, no. 2 (2011): 180–98.

14 Bethany E. Kok, Kimberly A. Coffey, Michael A. Cohn, Lahnna I. Catalino, Tanya Vacharkulksemsuk, Sara B. Algoe, Mary Brantley, and Barbara L. Fredrickson, "How Positive Emotions Build Physical Health: Perceived Positive Social Connections Account for the Upward Spiral between Positive Emotions and Vagal Tone," *Psychological Science* 24, no. 7 (2013): 1123–32.

15 David Comer Kidd and Emanuele Castano, "Reading Literary Fiction Improves Theory of Mind," *Science* 342, no. 6156 (2013): 377–80.

16   Imke Kirste, Zeina Nicola, Golo Kronenberg, Tara L. Walker, Robert C. Liu, and Gerd Kempermann, "Is Silence Golden? Effects of Auditory Stimuli and Their Absence on Adult Hippocampal Neurogenesis," *Brain Structure and Function* 220, no. 2 (2015): 1221–28.

17   Elizabeth Blackburn and Elissa Epel, *The Telomere Effect: A Revolutionary Approach to Living Younger, Healthier, Longer.* (New York: Grand Central Publishing, 2017).

18   Lan Nguyen Chaplin, Deborah Roedder John, Aric Rindfleisch, and Jeffrey J. Froh, "The Impact of Gratitude on Adolescent Materialism and Generosity," *Journal of Positive Psychology* (2018): 1–10, https://doi.org/10.1080/17439760.2018.1497688.

19   Y. Joel Wong, et al., "Does Gratitude Writing Improve the Mental Health of Psychotherapy Clients? Evidence from a Randomized Controlled Trial," *Psychotherapy Research* 28 (2018), 192–202.

20   Stephen R. Kellert and David J. Case, with Daniel Escher, Jessica Mikels-Carrasco, Phil T. Seng, and Daniel J. Witter, "The Nature of Americans: Disconnection and Recommendations for Reconnection," *The Nature of Americans National Report* (Mishawaka, IN: DJ Case & Associates, April 2017), https://natureofamericans.org/.

21   Peter A. Aspinall, Panagiotis Mavros, Richard Coyne, and Jenny Roe, "The Urban Brain: Analysing Outdoor Physi-

cal Activity with Mobile EEG," *British Journal of Sports Medicine* 49, no. 4 (2015): 272–76.

22 Paul K. Piff, Pia Dietze, Matthew Feinberg, Daniel M. Stancato, and Dacher Keltner, "Awe, the Small Self, and Prosocial Behavior," *Journal of Personality and Social Psychology* 108, no. 6 (2015): 883–99.

23 Diana I. Tamir, Emma M. Templeton, Adrian F. Ward, and Jamil Zaki, "Media Usage Diminishes Memory for Experiences," *Journal of Experimental Social Psychology* 76 (2018): 161–68.

24 Ken Goldberg, "The Robot-Human Alliance," *Wall Street Journal*, June 12, 2017.

Acknowledgments

Nothing happens in a vacuum. In physics, the opposite of a vacuum is called a plenum: a space entirely full of matter. Here are the incredible people that have mattered to me in the making of this book. It starts with Ken, my true love and best friend. He is always ready to collaborate, wrestle with an idea, and make me laugh. I appreciate his patience with my early nights so I could get up at dawn to write and for always being ready with a red pen to edit. Then to our daughters, Odessa and Blooma, who have been incredibly supportive: from Odessa's writing input and teenage perspective to Blooma bringing me a bell to ring after I finished writing each chapter and leaving little notes of encouragement for me to find on the printed pages. Thank you to my mother, Carole, a constant source of love in my life, whose passion for words, books, and psychology has been an inspiration; and to my sister, Kimberly, and brother, Jordan, for not only being there for me but also always pushing each other to live the height, width, and circumference of life. The model for that is our dad, who showed us, after being a surgeon for the first part of his life, that writing books could become an exciting way to distill and share ideas. Thank you to my mother-in-law, Ann, and stepmother, Ina, for their steady love and encouragement.

Thank you to my literary agents, Wendy Sherman and Nicki Richesin. You have guided me with grace and keen intelligence through this whole process. I love working with you both.

The next thank-you is to Vendela Vida and Rachel Lehmann-Haupt. How lucky I am to have such great friends also comprise our monthly writing group, the Investigative Poets. Our meetings over the last two years have been a wonderful source of feedback and support. A big thank-you to Sawyer Steele, who has been my consulting prefrontal cortex and filmmaking partner for almost fourteen years now. It was always a pleasure to come to the studio to share new chapters with you.

Odessa once said, "It sounds like you are having a baby when you talk about the book. People ask, 'When's the due date? What's the name?'" If that were the case, then the literary doula extraordinaire would be Jenny Traig, whom I have had the pleasure to work with for the last decade on films and my quarterly newsletter, and who served as developmental editor on this book. With the ping-pong of drafts back and forth and a lot of laughter and book therapy sessions in between, thank you for always being such a joy to work with.

Now onto the dream team at Simon & Schuster's Gallery Books. First, Karyn Marcus, my fantastic editor, for her unwavering focus on finding the right balance and for guiding the manuscript from words to an actual book. A thank-you to Cara Bedick, whose original belief in the book helped get it started. Thanks to Jen Bergstrom, my publisher, with so many ideas and energy; we were like electrons bouncing off each other when we met. Thank you for your great leadership at Gallery along with Aimee Bell and Jennifer Long. It is so clear how much the whole team enjoys working together and getting books out into the world. Many thanks to Jane Isay for her wisdom and perspective. Gratitude to Molly Gregory, Rebecca Strobel, and Sara Kitchen, who provided terrific editorial assistance. Special shout-out to Molly for her heroic support during deadlines. Many thanks to Caroline Pallotta for keeping everything on track. Thanks to Jean Anne Rose, Kathleen Carter, Abby Ziddle, and Tara Schlesinger for their elegant ideas and enthusiasm with helping to get the word out about the project.

Appreciation to John Vairo for the gorgeous "That's the one!" cover design; Una Lorenzen, who helped sketch out ideas when I first wanted to experiment with a color burst on the cover; Dave Eggers, who sat with me to play around with ideas; and to Debbie Millman, who gave me design counsel and a beautiful home away from home to stay in on my book trips to NYC.

To my whole posse of closest friends, thank you for always coming with gusto to any conversation or costume party. Those in particular who gave direct feedback on the book include: Maya Draisin, Amy and Gil Gershoni, Alan Eyzaguirre, Sydney Mintz, Tanya Selvaratnam, Julie Hermelin, Gina Pell, Nathan Shedroff, Amy Miller Gross, Jennifer Morla, and Zem and James Joaquin. Special thanks to my sisters-in-law, Elena Man and Adele Goldberg, for participating in our first retreat on Tech Shabbats and sharing their great insights.

Thanks to my father's book agent, Robert Stricker, who served as the literary godfather, giving advice and regaling me with stories of my father's adventures with publishing his books. Thank you to my lawyer, M. J. Bogatin, for his great counsel. Thanks to

Marc Geiger, who always encourages me to explore and create in all different mediums. My film directors' group, Film Fatales, who was there for me as I explored this new medium of only words on a page to convey everything I had normally expressed in films with words, images, and sound.

Thanks to Reboot, the unorthodox punk rock band of Jews who I get the pleasure of rethinking rituals and Jewish ideas with. Special thanks to Rabbi Amichai Lau-Levi, David Katznelson, Rachel Levin, Francine Hermelin, and Tanya Schevitz.

There was a wonderful period after I finished the first draft where I invited a wide range of people to read and give me notes. It was like what I would normally do for a film, a "rough cut" screening. It was intellectually boisterous, with layered comments that felt Talmudic, everyone coming from their different points of view. Thank you to: J Aguilar, Ariel Burger, Farai Chideya, David Dunkley Gyimah, Marc Engel, Brett Frischmann, Marina Gorbis, Dr. Jonathan Gray, Mimi Greisman, Janelle Hofmann, David Jaffe, Jasmine June, Rabbi Irwin Kula, Lisie Lillianfeld, Elena Man, Maya Man, Rabbi Sydney Mintz, Debbie Parker, Elizabeth Perlman, Howard Rheingold, Dr. Michael Rich, Beth Pettengill Riley, Delaney Ruston, Shaady Salehi, Richard Sergay, Brooke Shannon, Daniela Sirkin, Kevin Smokler, and Dirk Vom Lehn.

Thanks to Michael Larsen, Bruce Feiler, Susan Orlean, and Adam Fisher for sharing advice on the process of bookmaking.

Thanks to all those who shared their Shabbat experiences: Amy Emmerich and Colin Oberschmidt and family, Martin Rozenblum, Haim and Miriam Goldberg and family, Daniel Goldin, Vincent DeLuca, Jenn Lee and Lund Smith and family, Alan Eyzaguirre, Farai Chideya, Dorthe Eisele, Roy Hessel, and Casper ter Kuile.

ACKNOWLEDGMENTS

Thanks to Cissie Swig, Harlene Appleman, Joni Blinderman, Jackie Bezos, Sarah Clement, and Aaron Dorfman for helping share ideas from this book far and wide in the form of a global conversation for Character Day. Thanks to Geralyn Dreyfous, Jacki Zehner, Lauren Embrey, Ellen Friedman, Betsy Scolnik, Matthew Hiltzik, and Erik Lammerding for their long-standing support of my work around these themes.

Thanks to everyone whose research I've referenced, and the researchers who inspired them.

Thanks to my Jewish tradition, which invites questioning and evolving ideas all the time.

So, as I end the acknowledgments, I salute the plenum, full of everyone and everything that led to the creation of this book.

Which includes you, for reading and experiencing these ideas. Thank you.

To unplugging and the power of looking inward, upward, and forward.

About the Author

Honored by *Newsweek* as one of the "Women Shaping the 21st Century," Tiffany Shlain is an Emmy-nominated filmmaker and the founder of the Webby Awards. Her films and work have received more than eighty awards and distinctions, including being selected for the Albert Einstein Foundation's *Genius: 100 Visions for the Future*. NPR named Shlain's UC Berkeley address on its list of best commencement speeches, and her films have premiered at top festivals, including Sundance, and are used by the US State Department to foster dialogue at embassies globally. Shlain serves on the leadership board of the Center on Media and Child Health at Harvard's Boston Children's Hospital and the advisory board of the WaitUntil8th.org initiative to delay smartphones for kids, and is a Henry Crown Fellow of the Aspen Institute. For more than twenty years, she has published a quarterly newsletter about film, books, art, and tech called "Breakfast at Tiffany's." She and her husband and two children live in Northern California. Find out more about films, speaking, and newsletters at TiffanyShlain.com and follow on @tiffanyshlain.